Labor in the Boardroom

The Peaceful Revolution

by

James C. Furlong

DOW JONES BOOKS
PRINCETON, NEW JERSEY

Published by Dow Jones Books
P.O. Box 300, Princeton, NJ 08540

Printed and bound in the United States of America
10 9 8 7 6 5 4 3 2 1

Library of Congress Cataloging in Publication Data

Furlong, James, 1936-
Labor in the boardroom

Includes bibliographical references and index.
1. Employees' representation in management—Germany, West. 2. Employees' representation in management.
I. Title
HD5660.G4F85 658.31′52′0943 77-21441
ISBN 0-87128-537-1

Table of Contents

Introduction

Ever since World War II, West Germany has been leading a peaceful revolution in industrial relations. To an extent unmatched in the rest of the Western world, many German workers have been participating directly in corporate decision-making. As the process just now is evolving to include nearly all of the nation's big companies, workers not only are helping to decide such mundane matters as coffee-break provisions, they are also practically equal partners with management in such major matters as approving or rejecting big capital-spending projects.

This worker participation, or industrial democracy as it is frequently called, hasn't gone unnoticed in the rest of Western Europe. If such a system is successful in West Germany, with the economic and social stability there, it is bound to be tried out in neighboring countries. Thus, variations on Germany's theme are being played in Norway, Sweden, Holland, Denmark, Luxembourg and Austria. France and Britain are engaged in lively national debates on how to establish similar systems. And the Common Market itself has been working most of this decade to formulate minimum legal standards of worker participation to apply to the entire nine-nation bloc.

Although the U.S., up to this point at least, has been little touched by the worker-participation ideas, there are signs that this may be changing. U.S. labor unions generally have argued that labor has prospered within the existing American system of collective bargaining between parties that are fundamentally opposed in their interests. The AFL-CIO speaks openly of its fears that worker participation could weaken the traditional labor-capital adversary relationship and thereby the power of the unions.

But the United Auto Workers in 1976 made a first tentative move to embrace the idea of worker participation when it asked Chrysler Corp. to give the union two seats on Chrysler's board.

This proposal was inspired by an offer of Chrysler's United Kingdom subsidiary to let employees participate in the unit's decision-making. The UAW backed off when Chrysler management resisted the demand, but the union says it may well bring the idea up again. Whatever happens at Chrysler, the concept of worker participation will receive increasing attention in the U.S. in the years ahead.

Industrial-democracy concepts go beyond such ideas as "job enrichment" or the "humanization of work." The basic idea of industrial democracy is the extension of political democracy to economic life. Under this philosophy, labor is considered as necessary as capital to the functioning of a company.

In the background of the movement are the rising educational standards and political power of the working classes, the threat of communism in parts of Europe, the near chaos of labor relations in Britain and the pressures generated by surging energy costs.

Germany's industrial democracy concepts grew in the ashes of World War II. They were planted by German trade unionists and British occupation authorities, who vowed that the nation never again would fall into the dictatorial pattern of the Third Reich.

Since then, the German model has become the point of departure for industrial democracy programs elsewhere. German unions report visits from hundreds of foreigners seeking information about the German system, because it is the oldest and most extensive such system in any major Western nation.

Heightening the discussion around the world is West Germany's new law, effective July 1, 1976, widening the worker-participation arrangements that had spread gradually in the past 25 years. The law decrees that labor be given an equal number of seats with capital representatives on the supervisory boards of major German corporations, including some 40 subsidiaries of American corporations, such as Ford, General Motors, IBM and Procter & Gamble.

Many German businessmen still fear that worker participation is a prelude to socialism. Some communists consider it a hoax on the workers. But one of its leading proponents, Heinz Oskar Vetter, head of the German Trade Union Federation, considers it a step toward finding a "third way" between capitalism and communism.

Success or failure of the new German law will certainly have a strong impact on labor-capital relations throughout the West as industrialists contend with labor unrest, communist influence and the threat of nationalizations.

The German system, of course, is firmly rooted in the German society, and it may not be transferrable without considerable modifications. For one thing, the German unions are by and large prosperous and sympathetic to the profit motive. They have numerous business interests, including ownership of one of Germany's biggest banks, Bank für Gemeinwirtschaft. They are organized on modern industrial lines, with the German Trade Union Federation embracing 7.4 million of the total organized workforce of 8.6 million. By exerting powerful political influence through the Social Democratic Party, the unions have achieved a wide range of social-welfare legislation. They engage in a steady dialogue with government and industry on economic policy.

Not every country considering worker participation starts from such a favorable position. Countries like France long have been troubled by class warfare. Others like the U.S. have some unions that are riddled by violence and corruption. Britain not only is plagued by class warfare but also by an anachronistic union system in which as many as 20 union organizations may work, often at odds with each other, in the same company. The profit motive only recently has begun to find some friends among Italian leftist-dominated trade unionists.

For all this, however, the German example is making people in these countries think about how the basic ideas of worker participation might be adapted to their particular situations.

This book will attempt to examine the German model thoroughly—its warts as well as its beauty marks—and to relate this to efforts in other countries to give workers a greater voice in the operations of corporations.

Throughout this book, the reader will find a few German words and phrases that describe specific aspects of the industrial system there. The following glossary of words and phrases is intended to assist the reader.

Glossary

Aktiengesellschaft—joint stock company. Abbreviated as AG.

Angestellte—white-collar employee.

Arbeiter—blue-collar worker.

Arbeitsdirektor—management board member in charge of personnel.

Aufsichtsrat—supervisory board.

Betriebsrat—works council.

DGB (Deutscher Gewerkschaftsbund)—German Trade Union Federation

Leitende Angestellte—managerial white-collar employee.

Mitbestimmung—co-determination.

Montan—term used to describe coal, iron and steel industries.

Montanmitbestimmung—co-determination program in coal, iron and steel industries.

Vorstand—management board.

(In some cases, plurals have been anglicized.)

Chapter 1
Co-Determination: Rules of the Game

In almost any other Western nation, the legislation that took effect in West Germany in July 1976 would have caused a sensation. The measure gave workers a nearly equal voice with shareholders in controlling the affairs of 600 to 650 major companies, employing about five million people.

Yet the German public showed little reaction to the enactment of the measure, known as the Mitbestimmung Act (pronounced MIT-beh-SHTIH-mung) or Co-Determination Act.

Government spokesman Armin Grünewald attributed the widespread apathy to the public's failure to grasp the bill's vast implications. The learning process would take another ten years, he suggested. But Labor Ministry legislative authority Karl Fitting, head of the department that drafted the bill, went to the heart of the matter when he commented that the new measure was just the legislative expression of what already was "immanent in the system."

Indeed, the new act does represent only a moderate extension of an idea with 140 years of intellectual history and a quarter-century of successful practice in West Germany. Since 1951, the West German coal and steel industry, known as the montan industry, has been governed by a system of industrial relations that gives workers even more power than the new law requires. This arrangement, now covering some 600,000 montan workers, is unaffected by the new legislation.

Outside of the coal and steel industry, big companies in 1952 came under a regulation requiring that one-third of supervisory-board seats be allotted to labor. The 1976 law raises labor's participation in the largest companies to one-half.

Worker representation on companies' supervisory boards is the upper tier, so to speak, of German co-determination. It is designed to give workers early influence on strategic corporate decisions. The lower tier of co-determination consists of plant-level representation for workers on the so-called Betriebsrat, or works council.

The works councils, formally established in 1952 and strengthened in 1972, now must be established in practically all offices and plants. These councils have an equal voice with management in many aspects of hiring and firing, working conditions and other matters that have more immediate impact on the workers than top-level corporate decisions do.

The works councils so strongly limit traditional management prerogatives in these basic areas that Robert Lutz, the American-trained former management-board chairman of Ford Motor Co.'s German unit, spoke almost longingly during his German tour of duty about the U.S. "hire and fire" system.[1]

Labor unions play a strong role in both tiers of codetermination. The coal-steel Mitbestimmung arrangement (as well as the new law), guarantees a certain number of supervisory-board seats to union-selected representatives. Other labor representatives, selected by workers from within the company, are likely to be union members as well. At the plant level, the works councils, though formally separate from the unions, in practice are generally union-controlled and advised.

Works councils may not call strikes, although wildcat walkouts occur occasionally. Irreconcilable disputes between works councils and management in areas where the councils have codetermination rights are resolved either by an arbitration committee or a labor court. The labor courts have played a major role for decades in adjudicating worker grievances in Germany.

Unions can call strikes to back up collective bargaining demands after contracts expire, but labor and management seldom force showdowns because the government doesn't provide conciliation or arbitration services to help resolve bargaining impasses. Collective bargaining in Germany normally takes place annually between unions and regional associations that represent employers in particular industries.

German workers thus have several avenues to accomplish their aims: board-level participation, plant and office codetermination, and collective bargaining. Workers can also wield political influence through the Social Democratic Party. The net result of all this is that strikes are rare and short.

Mitbestimmung today functions in a system that has been

in effect in Germany's so-called joint stock companies since 1870. Under this system, immediate control of the company is split between the supervisory board (Aufsichtsrat) and management board (Vorstand).

As defined in the Joint Stock Company Act of 1965, the Aufsichtsrat has two main duties—to appoint (and, if necessary, fire) members of the management board, and to oversee the management board's work.

The German supervisory board sometimes is compared to the board of directors of American companies, while the management board is likened to the American management committee. The German system, unlike the American setup, however, doesn't allow anyone to belong to both bodies.

Supervisory-board members normally don't devote full time to the job. The board meets only four times a year as a rule, though board committees may convene more often, and individual members may be in frequent contact with members of the management board.

The size of the role given the supervisory board in corporate affairs differs from company to company. The board's legal duties often are supplemented by company bylaws that give the board veto power over major capital spending projects, closings or movements of plants, company bond issues and the appointment of upper-middle managers. Though the Aufsichtsrat may not take day-to-day management powers away from the Vorstand, it nevertheless may designate certain decisions as needing its approval. The supervisory board's success in exploiting this gray area depends on the aggressiveness, ingenuity, and personal strength of its members.

An example of the successful use of these powers was provided in April 1976 in connection with the decision of Volkswagenwerk AG to establish an assembly plant in the U.S. The government- and union-dominated VW supervisory board conditioned its approval of the project on management agreement to await the Aufsichtsrat's okay before increasing the percentage of U.S. components in American-assembled cars from the original 65%. The restriction was introduced at the insistence of the supervisory board's vice chairman, Eugen Loderer, head of the big I.G. Metall union, as a means of limiting the loss of jobs to the U.S.

The imposition of this condition and several others made some observers charge that management had abdicated its rights to the Aufsichtsrat. No one doubted the toughness of Management Board Chairman Toni Schmücker, but it was widely noted that Schmücker had learned the art of compromise thoroughly during his years as an executive of the strictly co-determined steel industry.

Company law gives the Vorstand the legal duty to run the day-to-day affairs of the company and to represent the company in dealings with third parties. The Vorstand is headed by a chairman, or in cases where the board likes to sound more democratic, by a "speaker." In either case, the leader is more a "first among equals" than a boss; the law doesn't allow him to overrule the majority of his Vorstand colleagues when disputes arise.

The Vorstand consists of highly paid executives who serve renewable terms of up to five years. Each Vorstand member has responsibility for a special area of company operation as well as a share of the responsibility for the company as a whole. The VW management board shows a typical profile for a major company. It consists of eight members, besides Chairman Schmücker. They are responsible, respectively, for personnel, public relations-economics-law, research and development, production, purchasing, sales, the Audi NSU subsidiary, and finance and administration.

The deep involvement of German Vorstand members in company affairs gives them a specialized knowledge that usually weights the scales in their favor when it comes to a contest of wills with the supervisory board. In addition, the Vorstand is entitled legally to appeal any Aufsichtsrat veto of its plans to a special meeting of the shareholders. The shareholders assembly may overrule such a veto with a three-quarter majority.

This possibility is more theoretical than actual because few Vorstands would care to put in motion the ponderous, noisy and expensive process of summoning a special meeting to resolve an interboard dispute. Gottfried Walther, chief of the legal department of the West German Industry Federation, said that in the history of montan industry co-determination, no meeting ever has been called for this purpose.

Walther said, however, that he knows of two occasions when a Vorstand threat to call a special meeting forced worker-directors (labor representatives on the supervisory boards) to back down on demands. The unions, he added, take the possibility of a special meeting seriously enough for some union strategists to have proposed diluting these shareholder powers.

The shareholder assembly has a number of rights besides the power to countermand Aufsichtsrat vetos. The assembly elects shareholder representatives to the Aufsichtsrat, and it has authority to approve or reject such things as mergers, uses of profits, capital changes and changes of direction by the company.

The Labor Ministry comments, however, that the "legal and actual influence of the general [shareholders] assembly in reality is much smaller than would be supposed on the basis of this comprehensive catalogue of formal rights. In practice, the Aufsichtsrat has a significantly stronger position than the general assembly."[2]

The Aufsichtsrat is the locus of worker power under the new law. Choice of this body for worker representation is intended to stress the supervisory, rather than management, character of worker participation.[3] The act stipulates that in virtually all companies (outside the steel and coal industries) that have more than 2,000 workers, labor representatives shall hold half the supervisory board seats, up from one-third prior to the new law.

This arithmetical parity is diluted, however, by a political compromise between the leftist Social Democratic Party and its centrist coalition partner, the Free Democratic Party. First, the law effectively guarantees that the Aufsichtsrat chairman always will represent capital, and it gives the chairman an extra vote to break deadlocks. Second, it assigns one worker seat to a representative of the so-called leitenden Angestellten, or upper-middle managers. This executive representative would seem to have everything to lose and nothing to gain by voting consistently with labor's representatives.

Given these features, it might appear that workers have been fobbed off with a sort of *Animal Farm* equality in which capital is "more equal" than Labor. Nominally, the 20-member Aufsichtsrat that is standard for the largest companies will comprise 10 worker representatives and 10 shareholder members. Look closer, the unions argue, and you see the board consists of 21 votes, 12 of which effectively belong to capital.

But the power shift effected by the law can't be judged alone by counting heads and votes. A number of unresolved issues will be crucial to the future balance of power. These questions, to be dealt with in detail later, include:

—What effect will increased union representation from outside the company have on the worker side of the Aufsichtsrat?

—Will the chairman be willing to risk conflict by exercising his deciding vote?

—How will the representative of the leitenden Angestellten vote?

—What are the implications of the law's seemingly harmless stipulation that each management board must have a personnel director?

—Could capital's slim voting edge sometimes be offset by the unexpected absence of a member from a meeting—if he is "caught in a traffic jam," to use a theoretical case cited by Hanns Martin Schleyer,* head of the West German Employers Association?

—Will the unions now push harder than ever to achieve their major postwar goal of true labor-capital equality?

The rules of the Mitbestimmung game help to provide insights into such questions. The 1976 law prescribes supervisory boards consisting of 12, 16, or 20 members, depending on the number of employees in the companies involved. Labor representatives are chosen by the workers themselves, or by the workers' electors, in a process so complex that the government's draft set of election instructions for implementing the law weighs over three pounds.

The law, for example, guarantees some board seats to persons nominated by trade unions, rather than by workers at the company involved. Many managers fear that these representatives, who generally will be union officials from outside the company, will become legally sanctioned "outside agitators."

Union-nominated representatives will be allotted two seats on boards that have either 12 or 16 members and three seats on boards with 20 members. This provision represents a major advance in union power. Under the previous Mitbestimmung law, which provided for one-third labor representation on supervisory boards, workers were free to choose outside unionists after filling the first two labor posts with candidates from within

*Hanns Martin Schleyer apparently was kidnapped in Cologne September 5, 1977. As this book went to press, his fate was unknown.

the company, but in practice the workers tended not to make much use of this opportunity.

The labor representatives that were chosen from within the company were usually union members, of course, but they tended not to have the immunity from employer reprisals that outsiders would have.

The 1976 law also gives at least one seat on the supervisory boards to each class of employees—the Arbeiter, or blue-collar workers, the Angestellten, or white-collar employes, and the leitenden Angestellten, or upper-middle managers. Generally, representation of the three classes is to be proportional to their numbers on a company's payroll; the provision for at least one seat guarantees representation for the leitenden Angestellten, who normally are a small minority in a company.

Once seated, the board elects one of its members to the key post of chairman by two-thirds majority vote. If no candidate gets two-thirds, separate votes are held on the labor and shareholder sides of the board, with labor electing the vice chairman and the shareholder side naming the chairman.

The procedure is intended to ensure that no worker representative will become chairman without the consent of the shareholders. This consent probably won't be forthcoming under foreseeable circumstances, so it can be assumed that the chairmanship—and thus the extra vote—will normally be in the hands of the shareholders.

The supervisory board elects members of the Vorstand, or management board, by two-thirds majority. If the necessary margin isn't achieved on the first vote, a four-member committee is given the task of coming up with an acceptable candidate. The committee, comprising two shareholder and two worker representatives, has one month to come up with a candidate suggestion.

After a month, the full board convenes again and votes anew. The committee's candidate, if the group has come up with one, doesn't exclude other suggestions. In this second vote, the candidate may be elected with a simple majority, rather than the two-thirds edge required on the first ballot.

The chairman may not cast his deciding ballot on the second vote. Thus, if the two sides remain deadlocked in the second vote, a third election is necessary. Only at this point may the chairman cast his vote to win the day for the capital side.

This complex three-vote procedure is limited to the crucial

task of selecting Vorstand members. For other business, decision is by majority vote. If no majority is obtained, the chairman casts his deciding vote on the second ballot, assuming he is willing to risk antagonizing the labor side by overruling it.

But employers worry about the voting procedure. Suppose, they say, that a capital representative unexpectedly fails to show up at a meeting without sending in an absentee ballot. In such a case, the matter could be decided on the first vote in labor's favor. The chairman may not cast his extra vote unless a tie exists; he may not cast the second vote to *create* a tie.

The employers associations aren't at all convinced that the upper-middle managers on the labor side will prevent cases like this from occurring by voting consistently with capital. Schleyer of the employers association notes that fellow worker representatives might make life difficult for a representative of the leitenden Angestellten who lets the worker side down. An industry-association specialist contends that upper-middle managers have been exposed to socialist thought ever since the German left in the late 1960s began a "march through the institutions"—an attempt to win influence in the schools, media and churches. "Who's to guarantee that the leitenden Angestellten will vote with capital?" he asks.

The controversy that has arisen over the creation of a special Vorstand post for a personnel manager may appear puzzling at first glance. The provision may seem harmless enough from capital's viewpoint. Most large companies already have such a post, although smaller concerns often delegate personnel matters to a lower-level manager. The post certainly doesn't, ipso facto, require a pro-labor man; the personnel manager at Daimler-Benz AG until recently was none other than Hanns Martin Schleyer, the conservative chief of the West German Employers Association.

The controversy stems from the title given to the personnel director. The title—"Arbeitsdirektor"—is the same as that of the personnel manager in coal and steel industry companies. In these companies the Arbeitsdirektor may not be chosen over the veto of the labor side of the supervisory board. This veto power in practice has led to nearly total union control of the post of Arbeitsdirektor.

The new law contains no such veto provision, but the use of the term "Arbeitsdirektor" in the law was a clear signal to the

DETERMINING THE NUMBER OF JOBHOLDERS
IN A CONTROLLING COMPANY

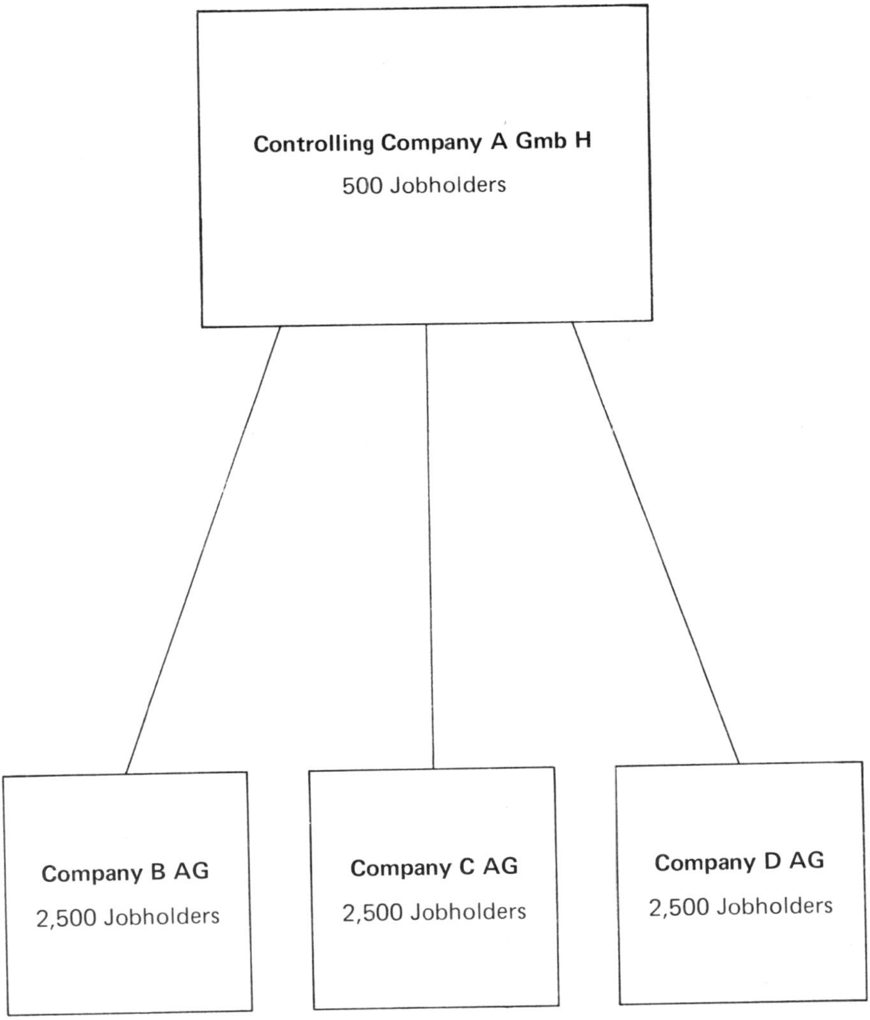

Controlling Company A has a co-determined board under the new law, although it has only 500 jobholders. The new law counts the jobholders of Companies B, C, and D as part of Company A's workforce. (Companies B, C, and D also have co-determined boards under the new law).

unions to strive for de facto control of the position. The unions were quick to pick up the signal. Union success would please the Social Democrats and anger the Free Democrats; the two parties in the government coalition have quarreled publicly about the point.

Whether all this means that German workers have in their board-level, plant-level and collective-bargaining powers a position of near-equality with capital, or even a slight edge over shareholders is a matter for ideologues of the right and left to argue. What is clear is that German workers enjoy more legal corporate decision-making power than their counterparts in any other major Western industrialized nation.

Just how they use this clout won't become clear immediately. The law allows a transition period of two years, ending July 1, 1978, for companies to create "parity" boards. An additional one to three years will be needed to see how workers, unions, management and shareholders react to the new order of things. But the German experiment is certain to affect labor relations throughout the Western world.

How did Germany happen to be a pioneer industrial democracy?

Hanns Martin Schleyer, echoing a frequent charge of ideological opponents, says Mitbestimmung was a "gift of the British occupation forces."[4] It is hard to imagine a more devastating charge. A German may buy a Rolls-Royce, but hardly a system of labor relations that was "Made in Britain"—the nation that has horrified the world with its "I'm All Right Jack" worker-management quagmire.

But the historical record shows that although Schleyer's charge has some merit, it tells only half the story. The introduction of Mitbestimmung in the Ruhr-area steel industry shortly after World War II was a joint effort of the German unions and the British military occupation government, which was responsible for the Ruhr region.

History provides no justification for any suggestion that Mitbestimmung was an alien idea forced upon a prostrate Germany by ruthless victors. However, German industrialists acceded to the Mitbestimmung initiatives of the unions and military government only under duress.

Mitbestimmung in anything resembling its present form goes back to 1919, when Article 165 of the new Weimar Constitution laid the groundwork for works councils and worker representation on company supervisory boards. But the general concept of worker participation goes back as far as the 1830s, long before the fateful 1860s when the German union movement started and Karl Marx published *Das Kapital*.

Information supplied by the German Labor Union Federation traces the participation idea to Robert von Mohl, a liberal law professor in Tübingen and Heidelberg, who proposed in 1835 joint negotiations of employers and worker groups on employees suggestions for improvement of working conditions.[5] The German Labor Ministry notes that the 1848 Frankfurt Constitutional Assembly debated a measure that would have established factory committees with powers to participate in owners' decision-making processes. Though the discussion didn't result in legislation, worker committees were set up on a voluntary basis in some companies in following years.

In 1905, the Prussian Mining Law ordered the establishment of worker committees in mining companies with more than 100 employees. The social-liberal parliamentary deputy, Friedrich Naumann, spearheaded a drive to widen the system, but the effort was dropped in 1910 after several draft laws failed to obtain Reichstag approval.

World War I provided the next big push for worker participation. As defeat loomed for the Kaiser's armies in 1916, the government enacted the Fatherland Auxiliary Service Law, decreeing that working councils be formed in all war-related plants with more than 50 employees. The councils had the right to make their views known to management on personnel matters and working conditions, but they didn't have any voice in final decisions.

In the turmoil that followed the war, some leftists argued for the creation of a society based on worker councils rather than on parliamentary democracy. They lost out on this demand, but councils were given a prominent place in the Weimar Constitution of 1919.[6]

The government used the Constitution's Article 165 as the basis for enactment of legislation in 1920 establishing works councils in factories with more than 19 workers. The councils had a strong voice in companies' social, personnel and economic affairs.

Another precedent-setting postwar law ordered in 1922 that companies having supervisory boards give at least one seat on this panel to a work-council member. And the DGB asserts that in the mid-1920s, the Prussian State Mining and Smelting Co.—predecessor of today's privately owned Preussag AG—introduced on its management board one personnel director endorsed by the workers and unions. The position was analogous to the current-day "Arbeitsdirektor" in the steel and coal industries.[7]

The Nazi power seizure in 1933 put an end to meaningful works councils and unions. The Nazi "Law for the Arrangement of National Work" dissolved works councils. Troops occupied union headquarters and confiscated their funds. Leading trade unionists were placed under "protective" arrest. Lesser union members, along with employers, were thrust into a new association called the German Work Front. Worker participation gave way to Hitler's "Führer Principle."

Among those arrested was a 58-year-old former silver and gold industry worker named Hans Böckler, who had risen to a seat in the Reichstag through the union movement and who had served as secretary of the Central Work Society, a short-lived effort to bring about union-industry cooperation on national policy questions after World War I.

Following his arrest, Böckler was tried on Nazi charges in 1934 but acquitted and released to spend the rest of the "Nazizeit" dodging government harassment. He went into hiding in 1944 but emerged following the war with a plan for transforming German society and decisively eradicating any lingering adherence to the "Führer Principle."

In a March 1946 speech at Hannover before the first union conference in the British Zone, Böckler declared:

"We must . . . be represented in the economy with fully equal rights. . . . Therefore, the thought is: representation in management and supervisory boards of companies."[8]

The national mood was ripe for big changes. In a postwar speech reflecting the spirit of the times, Chancellor-to-be Konrad Adenauer said: "The private capitalistic monopoly economy hasn't done justice to the national and social vital interests of the German people. An unheard-of economic and social collapse was the consequence of the power policy that was followed. . . . The German economy can't be repaired. It must be newly ordered from the ground up."[9]

German trade unionists, as well as the British occupation government, were actively considering the idea that basic industries should be nationalized. The movement toward state ownership was given increased impetus by the nationalization process underway under the Labor Government in Great Britain.

Unions and Ruhr industrialists met in May 1946 at Düsseldorf to discuss this theme. The industrialists resisted union suggestions for state ownership, but agreed German company law should guarantee the "responsible participation of members of a plant in its development."[10]

In August 1946, direction of the Ruhr-area steel companies was taken over by the British military occupation and given to the North German Iron and Steel Control Board as a step toward decartelization, one of the aims of the Potsdam Agreement. Faced with these pressures, major steel companies—including Hagen Haspe, Gütehoffnungshütte, Vereinigtestahlwerke and Klöckner—began agreeing to union demands for parity representation on supervisory boards. Their hope was that union leaders, who had the ear of the British occupation authorities, would prevent the decartelization process from wrecking the German steel industry.

The board-level Mitbestimmung taking hold in the Ruhr steel industry ran parallel to the movement to reestablish works councils throughout the conquered land. Allied Control Council Law No. 22 of April 1946 provided the legal framework for their development.

Herbert Baker, a U.S. diplomat specializing in labor relations who was in Germany during the immediate postwar period, recalled: "Americans were surprised when German unionists whose democratic credentials were impeccable because they'd been persecuted during the war asked for a works-council law. Many Americans felt works councils would compete with unions. But as a matter of policy the U.S. wanted to go along with democratic elements, so the Allied Control Council allowed them. But the law was loose. It didn't have the Roman-law type of precision associated with German legislation."

Baker noted that the Americans wanted the Germans to use collective bargaining to fill in the purposely created gaps in the law. But the German penchant for precision wasn't to be denied, and the current works-council legislation is highly detailed, leaving relatively little to negotiation.

With board-level Mitbestimmung established in the Ruhr and with works councils flourishing throughout the economy, worker co-determination was well established when the military government gave way in 1949 to the new Federal Republic of Germany. Earlier discussion of nationalization had died down. But the translation of the co-determination system into German law wasn't easy.

From the unions' point of view, the government must have appeared headed in the right direction in the autumn of 1949 when Chancellor Konrad Adenauer, a conservative Christian Democrat, spoke in his first government address of the necessity for altering the "legal relationships between employees and employers."[11]

But the unions were incensed when in 1950 the Christian Democrats, and their Bavarian sister party, the Christian Social Union, presented a draft Mitbestimmung law that envisaged only one-third worker participation in company supervisory boards. The bill obviously fell short of union demands for parity on boards of all major German companies and for the right to approve nominations for the Vorstand post of Arbeitsdirektor.

More importantly, the bill threatened to reduce the already won gains in the Ruhr steel industry. The unions responded in November 1950 by demanding parity Mitbestimmung throughout the steel industry as well as its extension to the mining sector.

The I.G. Metall union, representing some 210,000 iron and steel workers, scheduled a strike authorization vote in November 1950 to protest the bill. Two days prior to the vote, Adenauer wrote to Hans Böckler challenging the planned strike vote on legal grounds. Adenauer contended that unions were permitted to strike only to back up contract demands, not to push political goals.[12]

Adenauer wrote: "Such a strike could only have the goal of using economic damage or the threat of it to channel the decision of the freely elected [parliamentary] representatives of the people in the direction of union wishes."

Böckler didn't back down; the strike vote was carried out. Nearly 96% of the participants authorized a strike. Reinforced by the vote, Böckler wrote back to Adenauer. Though he used constitutional grounds to justify a possible strike, the heart of his letter was philosophical and political, rather than legal.

He said: "The German unions are of the view that the general world political development shows that only through a viable social order can totalitarianism and the loss of individuality be stopped. They are further of the opinion that it is vitally important for democracy in Germany that democracy shouldn't remain confined to the political area but that it should receive its obvious completion through the introduction of democratic principles in economic leadership and structure. The unions see the proof of their interpretation in the fact of the misuse of economic power to political ends in the past and in the mournful consequences of this misuse—namely, war and destruction."

The struggle was heating up. On Jan. 3, 1951, I.G. Metall scheduled a strike for Feb. 1. I.G. Bergbau, the mining union, called a vote Jan. 17 to 19 that produced a strike authorization by a 92.5% majority.

Adenauer saw the handwriting on the wall. The new government, faced with high unemployment and eager to get on with the reconstruction, couldn't afford a strike in the basic industries. Adenauer initiated negotiations between unions and employer federations that led on Jan. 25 to agreement in principle that parity Mitbestimmung would be given legal status in the steel and coal industries throughout the country.

In a radio speech Jan. 30, the victorious Böckler expressed satisfaction with the new compromise but promised it was only the beginning of an economic reordering that would lift the worker out of his historical role of dependency. On Feb. 16, Böckler died of a heart attack, ten days short of his 76th birthday.

The "Montanmitbestimmung" bill passed the Bundestag April 10 and went into effect May 21. From the unions' point of view, the measure marked a high-water point in the Mitbestimmung movement. They have worked unceasingly ever since to get a system like Montanmitbestimmung spread throughout the country. They have come close.

The essential feature of Montanmitbestimmung is that it creates a labor-capital relationship on supervisory boards that is probably as close to equality as possible. But because "true parity is possible only in Heaven," as Karl Fitting of the Labor Ministry comments, the law makes one inconsequential concession to capital, which will be described later.

The 1951 law, embracing all steel and coal companies with more than 1,000 workers, prescribes a supervisory board of 11, 15 or 21 members, depending on the nominal amount of the share capital of the company involved.

The 11-member board, for example, consists of five labor representatives, five shareholder representatives and one neutral member who in theory casts the deciding vote in case of a deadlock.

The shareholder side consists of four members appointed by the general shareholder assembly without any restriction. The fifth member representing the shareholders must be independent of capital and workers and their organizations.

The composition of the labor side is more complex. The five-member labor team must consist of at least two company jobholders—one blue collar and one white collar—and three other members, nominated by the unions, who need not come from within the company.

The jobholder-representatives are nominated and elected by the blue-collar and white-collar members of the works council acting as separate groups. The unions may object to any jobholder chosen. If the works council affirms its choice in the face of such an objection, the council or the union may appeal to the Labor Minister, whose decision is final.

The unions, after consulting with works councils, nominate the other three members, one of whom must be independent in the same sense that the fifth member of the shareholder side is independent. The shareholder assembly formally approves the worker side, but the recommendations of workers and unions are binding on the assembly.

An unwritten agreement in most montan companies gives shareholder members of the Aufsichtsrat the privilege of nominating the board chairman. The labor side in turn nominates the neutral member, explains Hans-Adam Pfromm, Mitbestimmung expert of the I.G. Metall union.

Should the general assembly refuse to accept the nomination for the neutral member, the law provides for lengthy conciliation and court procedures that ultimately give the shareholders the balance of power.

It works like this:

A committee of two labor and two capital board members deliberates and comes up with the names of three new nominees. If the assembly refuses to accept any of these, the local court of appeal determines whether the rejection was justified. If the rejection is held to be unjustified, the general assembly must elect one of the three nominees. If the rejection is ruled justified, the committee must come up with three new names. If the committee doesn't submit a new list or if the new list is rejected and the rejection is upheld by the court, the general assembly elects the neutral member on its own. If the rejection of the second list of candidates is ruled unjustified, the assembly must elect one of the three names on the second list.

Because it is unlikely that any shareholder assembly would go through this tortuous process, the theoretical ultimate edge of the shareholder assembly has only a limited effect.

Adenauer himself took a personal hand in formulating this complex procedure, Fitting noted. In an aside, Fitting recalled that he had the temerity to object to Adenauer's use of the word "should"—soll, in German—in one passage on the ground that the word was too vague. Adenauer shot back, "Young man, that is not a 'should' (soll)! That is a duty (Soll)!"

The other main feature of the montan law is the previously mentioned installation of an Arbeitsdirektor on the Vorstand. The Arbeitsdirektor may not be appointed against the wishes of a majority of labor representatives.

Having given in to a strike threat and legislated parity Mitbestimmung in the steel and coal industries, Parliament stood firm against union pressures for the extension of this high-powered form of co-determination to other industries.

Instead, Parliament passed in 1952 a two-part "Works Constitution Act" giving workers one-third representation on boards of other non-montan companies and providing a German legislative foundation for the works council system that was started under Occupation law.

Board-level Mitbestimmung under the 1952 law applied to most companies with more than 500 employees. It remains in effect following passage of the 1976 law for concerns with 500 to 2,000 jobholders; about a million jobholders continue to be affected by this arrangement.

Under the 1952 law, shareholder representatives hold two-thirds of the seats on supervisory boards, with the remainder going to worker deputies. The size of the board isn't fixed by this measure, but the 1965 Joint Stock Company law sets a minimum size of three.

The makeup of the jobholder side is straightforward: On supervisory boards with one or two labor representatives, each must be a company employee. In the case of a two-member labor side, one must be a blue-collar and one a white-collar employee. The worker deputies are chosen in direct general elections.

There isn't any restriction on who may occupy additional labor seats on larger boards, but in practice such seats have tended to go to company jobholders, rather than union outsiders.

One-third representation generally limited workers to a consultative, rather than co-determining, role on supervisory boards. Even this function often was undermined by shareholder representatives who shifted pre-decision planning to supervisory board committees from which workers were excluded.

But the sections of the 1952 law officially creating the Betriebsrat, or works council, involved a substantial transfer to workers of traditional management prerogatives. The works council legislation, as revised in 1972, gives workers a major voice in such matters as hiring and firing, job classifications, transfers, layoffs, overtime, short-time, safety and health, introduction of new equipment and vocational training.

Under the law, works councils are to be established in all plant and office facilities with five or more workers. A separate law covers civil service. Members are chosen by the workers from their own ranks, with blue-collar and white-collar jobholders voting separately unless they agree otherwise.

The councils, which are formally independent of the unions, may not strike or order slowdowns. The law requires the council and employers to meet together once a month and to make a constructive effort to solve labor-management issues. These issues don't include basic wages (for which a regional agreement normally is negotiated by central-union organizations and employers associations) but often involve extra payments above the basic wage.

When the council and employers can't agree, the most common procedure is to refer the dispute to an arbitration committee consisting of an equal number of jobholder and employer representatives plus one neutral member.

All costs of works council operations—office space, materials and transportation—are borne by the employer. Employers are required to release a certain number of council members from normal work while they handle council affairs at full pay. The number varies from one member in facilities with 300 to 600 employees, to 11 members in facilities with 9,001-10,000 workers. Beyond 10,000 workers, the number of council members released rises by one for each additional 2,000 jobholders. These are minimum figures; special agreements may provide for higher numbers in individual companies.

A significant right of works councils is to be given early information on planned major changes that could affect worker interests. The law requires employers to brief councils on plans for major reorganizations, closings of whole plants or major parts of plants, shifts of facilities to another site, and introduction of entirely new work methods and production processes.

In such cases, employers and works councils are directed by the law to come to an agreement on means for easing hardships on workers. If they fail to agree, the task falls to the arbitration committee or a labor court.

A successful agreement of this type was achieved at Volkswagenwerk when management reduced the domestic work force to 95,000 persons in mid-1975 from about 122,000 a year earlier. The reduction involved no firings. Instead the work force was cut by a combination of early pensioning of older workers, a stop on new and replacement hiring and bonuses for employees who quit voluntarily.

Besides giving councils powers to deal with personnel emergencies arising from major corporate changes, the law also deals with everyday company operations. The works council has, for example, an equal voice with the employer in setting guidelines for recruiting of new employees, transfers, assigning of workers to a new type of job, and dismissals, as well as powers to challenge violations of the guidelines.

The council acts as watchdog on changes in job content and work environment. If employers ignore established procedures of "ergonomics" (tailoring jobs to human requirements of workers), the council may ask for changes or for compensation to disadvantaged laborers. Unresolvable arguments are settled by the arbitration committee.

Other matters in which workers may force the issue to the arbitration committee include: treatment of individual workers' grievances, introduction of overtime or short-time, general principles for vacations, safety and health of workers, bonus rates, assignment of company housing, and appointment of vocational-training instructors and the choice of workers to participate in the training programs.

Works council economic committees meet with employer representatives once a month to get the latest information on companies' economic and financial condition, production and marketing situations, investment plans and any other matters that might affect worker well-being.

This account of works council rights and functions isn't exhaustive (and some of the rights apply only in larger companies). But it should help illustrate Karl Fitting's observation that works-council Mitbestimmung is "more in the life of the average worker" than is board-level co-determination. It also should make clear that German bosses would have to contend with considerable worker power even if board-level Mitbestimmung didn't exist.

Despite the long union dissatisfaction with the one-third co-determination system introduced in 1952, the cause of Mitbestimmung was little advanced in the next 15 years. There were a couple of exceptions. In 1955, the federal government introduced a law establishing civil-service personnel councils with certain participation rights in government decisions affecting federal employees. The law was complemented by similar measures affecting state employees. Then, in 1956, coal and steel industry parity Mitbestimmung was extended to cover holding companies that owned concerns primarily engaged in steelmaking and coalmining. The law was considered necessary because the montan industry, broken up under the Potsdam Agreement, had begun to reconcentrate.

The main reason for the dearth of movement in Mitbestimmung in the 1953-1968 period was that the Social Democratic Party, the German party with the closest ties to the unions, lacked political power. Until late 1966, the party had been excluded from the government altogether. When the Social Democrats did become part of the government in December 1966, it was as junior member of a coalition with the conservative parties.

Not until October 1969 did the political constellation become favorable for an extension of Mitbestimmung. It was then that the Social Democratic Party—a formerly Marxist reformist group that converted in 1959 to a philosophy of welfarism based on a free-market economy—formed a coalition with the centrist Free Democratic Party. On Oct. 28, 1969, new Chancellor Willy Brandt, a Social Democrat, announced the coalition's intention to widen Mitbestimmung.

The first concrete fulfillment of this goal was the Works Constitution Act of January 1972 that granted more powers to works councils. The new act replaced all parts of the 1952 Works Constitution Act with the exception of the section on board-level worker representation, which was left unchanged.

The political task of strengthening worker powers at board level was far more difficult than that of enlarging labor rights in the office and on the shop floor. The main obstacles to quick action were the differing concepts for Mitbestimmung of the Social Democrats and Free Democrats. Both parties advocated "equality" for labor, but the Social Democrats' version appeared more radical than the Free Democrats' ideas.

Specifically, the Social Democrats advocated the widening of Montanmitbestimmung throughout the society. This model, as previously noted, creates practically complete equality and assures unions a strong voice on company boards. The Free Democrats on the other hand, advocated a system offering no guaranteed places to outside union representatives and giving substantial representation to upper-middle managers. The Free Democrats' model, adopted in a fall 1971 party conference at Freiburg, was intended for use throughout the economy, including the steel and coal industries, where it would have replaced Montanmitbestimmung.

The divergent conceptions of the coalition partners came together briefly in February 1974, when the cabinet put forward a compromise Mitbestimmung bill for the consideration of Parliament. Announcing the bill, Chancellor Brandt said it embodied "the principle of effective equal rights for capital and labor in a degree that has been achieved neither in our land up to now nor in other Western countries."[13]

But the bill designed to satisfy everyone quickly proved to be anathema to everyone. Its key feature was a puzzling lack of instructions on how to break deadlocks on the supervisory board. The bill did give the shareholders' assembly the theoretical ultimate right to resolve disputes over the selection of Vorstand members, but it was silent as to how other supervisory board standoffs were to be settled. Shareholders argued the bill would stymie corporate decision-making.

One pro-capital opponent, Frankfurt attorney Martin Peltzer, wrote, "Co-determination in this form . . . is a German disease with a lot of 'Weltanschauung' [philosophy or ideology]; as one banker puts it, it is rather Wagnerian, and certainly has the very obvious look of the come-to-power ambition of the labor unions."[14]

Labor objected to the ultimate right of shareholders to choose Vorstand members and to the bill's guarantee of one supervisory board seat for a middle manager.

Foreign businessmen weighed in with sharp criticism. The American Chamber of Commerce in Germany—representing most of the big U.S. business and industrial interests in Germany—charged in the fall of 1974 that the measure would deprive shareholders of control over their property in violation of a 1954 German-American trade treaty.

The charge produced a sharp response from Vetter of the labor federation. He told a Hamburg audience in October 1974, "We in Germany don't live in a banana republic. Colonialism in Europe is dead, and the sooner they [American businessmen] see this, the better for all."[15]

But the American Chamber had aimed at a vulnerable point in the new law—its possible disregard for shareholder property rights. German employers were making similar complaints, based not on international treaties but on property-protection provisions of the German Constitution itself.

The coalition, nervous about these attacks, called hearings late in 1974 to thrash out constitutional aspects of the bill thoroughly. The hearings did nothing to allay the fears that the bill might be vulnerable to a constitutional challenge. The anxieties were intensified early in 1975, when the constitutional court in Karlsruhe struck down a government move to liberalize abortion law. What happened to the abortion measure could also happen to Mitbestimmung, party strategists reasoned. Legislative experts went back to the drawing boards.

It wasn't until December 1975 that the Social Democrats and Free Democrats came up with a mutually acceptable compromise that would reduce chances of an attack on constitutional grounds by giving shareholders a voting majority while maintaining a form suggesting labor-capital equality. The December compromise passed the Bundestag in March 1976 and went into effect on July 1, 1976.

The Free Democrats were extremely pleased with the bill. But the Social Democrats' outspoken research minister, Hans Matthöfer, termed the measure "lousy," while conceding it was the best available under the existing political conditions.[16]

Hanns Martin Schleyer, speaking for the employers, said the law would alter Germany's economic structure, shifting more power to the unions. A constitutional challenge would be considered, he said, adding that employers would have to bear with the law for the time being at least.[17]

The American Chamber of Commerce in Germany said it could "live with" the law.[18] Heinz Oskar Vetter of the labor federation said that despite the new law, the unions intend to continue to make their No. 1 demand the extension throughout the economy of the stronger Montanmitbestimmung system.[19]

American labor leader Samuel Gompers summed up the philosophy of U.S. unions in one word—"More!" The word crystallizes the American unions' pragmatic, non-ideological, bread-and-butter approach to labor-capital issues.

No such neat summary of German labor aims is available. German union leaders tend to express themselves less pungently and more ideologically than Gompers in framing their No. 1 demand, the strengthening of Mitbestimmung.

In most of the abundant polemical literature written by German unions to forward the cause of co-determination, the vocabulary appears better suited to the philosophy or sociology seminar than the factory. There is, in fact, a great deal of "Weltanschauung" wrapped up in Mitbestimmung.

But if the demands had to be reduced to a Gompers-style slogan, it might be: "More democracy."

The fundamental tenet of Mitbestimmung advocates is that democracy cannot be limited to the political sphere but must be extended to economic life as well. Chancellor-to-be Helmut Schmidt provided a good sample of this view in a Bundestag speech in January 1969. He noted that his Social Democratic Party wrote in its basic program framed at Bad Godesberg in 1959 that the worker must be converted from an "economic vassal" into an "economic citizen."

He explained this declaration by saying that society can't over the long run tell workers these two contradictory things:[20]

"In political life, you have equal rights because you can, for example, co-determine in Bundestag elections who should be your government's chief, and because your vote will carry exactly as much weight as the vote of any other citizen of this country. In your work, things are different. You have a lower rank than the others." He added, "Over the long run, no one will understand that."

The theme of extending to economic life the principles of political democracy—the right of all citizens to help choose their leaders and to express their opinions freely on the choice and fulfillment of group goals—is the red thread that runs through all defenses of Mitbestimmung.

The German obsession with more democracy is understandable in light of the nation's catastrophic experience with the Nazi dictatorship from 1933 to 1945. Heinz Oskar Vetter goes so far as to blame the lack of economic democracy for the Nazi holocaust. Vetter said in a speech in October 1975:

"Far-seeing liberals like Friedrich Naumann recognized in the framing of the Weimar Constitution the necessity of resolving the contradiction between political citizen and economic vassal . . . (His) concept was only partly realized in the Weimar Constitution. The consequences are known."[21]

The labor federation in a 1968 tract commented: "Influential business leaders [in the period 1918-1933] misused economic power by contributing significantly to the rise of National Socialism and therefore to the fall of the Weimar Republic. Hardship arising from the abuse of economic power as political power or social power must be borne steadily by the workers. In order to prevent misuses of such power against individuals, against groups, against society, in order to prevent these as much as possible, the sources of power—the big companies—must be controlled. Therefore, the call for Mitbestimmung."[22]

Vetter advanced the same argument in a Bundestag committee hearing in October 1974 when he said:

"One of the first and most important reasons for our demand for Mitbestimmung was the experience with the 'Führer Principle' of National Socialism. . . . "[23]

Political democracy in the U.S. Constitution is justified by the recognition that "All men are created equal." The analogy for economic democracy is the assertion that labor and capital are equal because both are equally necessary to carry out productive work. This assertion stops short of the Marxist belief that labor is the source of all value, but it nonetheless is radical in its own way.

The argument goes that no company can function without workers any more than it can operate without capital. Capitalists contribute money to the company; workers contribute half their waking lives.

If it is argued that capital deserves higher status because shareholders take risks on the future of the company, Mitbestimmung proponents will answer that workers stake their entire livelihoods and careers on the firm.

Peter Frerk, personnel director of Volkswagenwerk AG, alludes to the human-value arguments for Mitbestimmung when he says, "You can get money from Zürich in a night call in three minutes. It's also easy to get nuts and bolts. But you can't shift human existence like hardware."

The real question facing employers today isn't whether to give workers power or withhold it. Workers in modern industrial society have great power already, and the problem is how to channel it constructively. German proponents of Mitbestimmung hold that co-determination of the issues at the conference table is better than "co-determination by strike," to quote Vetter again.[24]

Professor Karl Otto Hondrich, sociology professor at the University of Frankfurt, has said, "If there were no Mitbestimmung, then the relative growth in contribution and power of workers would have to be felt in another form in company decision-making processes. This we observe to some extent in the Anglo-Saxon and Italian forms of worker controls."[25]

Frerk of Volkswagenwerk suggests another advantage of Mitbestimmung. "In France, the owners have 100% authority," he said during an interview. "But last week a Frenchman sat in the chair you're occupying right now and said to me, 'We have no relations with the workers. They're rising, and we have no contact with them. How can we tame them a little?' "

Mitbestimmung apparently does have a "taming" effect on German workers, though this is just a byproduct. The low German strike rate is the envy of the U.S. and European countries.

Work days lost through strikes and lockouts per 1,000 jobholders in 1975, based on the size of the work force in 1974:

U.S.	363
West Germany	3
Belgium	192
Denmark	52
France	205
Great Britain	261
Ireland	742*
Italy	1,488
Netherlands	0.1

*1974 figure

Sources: U.S. Bureau of Labor Statistics, European Economic Community. Figures supplied by U.S. Embassy, Bonn, and German Federal Press Office.

The ability of German salesmen to make long-term production commitments well in advance without having to worry about strike-caused delivery delays has taken many a choice bit of business away from their French, Italian and British counterparts.

Hans-Adam Pfromm of the I.G. Metall Union put it this way: "In the steel industry, we have the classic worker. He is left-oriented. But he is satisfied. That's because conflicts are resolved steadily, not once a year. There are no revolutions in truly co-determined companies."

Pfromm conceded that Communists tend to regard Mitbestimmung as a form of hoax on the workers, but he shrugged this off. "The union movement is revisionist in any case," he said. "It wants immediate gains for the worker. If that leads to a good relationship with capital, we don't refuse it. However, we at I.G. Metall don't speak of a 'partnership with capital' but of 'close cooperation between conflict parties.' "

Against these theoretical and practical arguments for Mitbestimmung, opponents cite a variety of philosophical and legal objections, some of which already have been noted. The main objections, reduced to slogans, might be stated thus: "Democracy is a political and not an economic matter. And too many cooks spoil the broth."

Ruppert Siemon, managing director of the German Protection Association for Securities Ownership in Düsseldorf, feels it's a conceptual mistake to try to transfer the idea of political democracy to industrial and business life. The two realms are different, he asserted. For example, he added, "Democracy lives from the change of power. Industry lives from steadiness."

More concretely, he asserted, "There is no communist or capitalist steel. There is only good steel and bad steel. In our society, we must have enough capital to make good steel and pay enough dividends to get shareholder investments." Referring to the human aspects of Mitbestimmung, he said, "Teamwork—the avoidance of unilateral decisions—has been practiced in industry for decades. We don't need any politically motivated Mitbestimmung for this."

The "too-many-cooks" argument holds that Mitbestimmung blurs the clear line of authority that allows companies to take the swift, hard decisions necessary to survive and remain competitive in domestic and foreign markets. Managements that are subject to workers' review function slowly and make compromises in response to pressure from the Aufsichtsrat above and the works council below, it's argued.

Managers and ambitious junior executives working in co-determined industries must cater to workers and trade unionists to ensure their futures, another argument runs. To do this, they must neglect the welfare of the company.

Opponents concede that Mitbestimmung hasn't wrecked the German steel industry. But they argue that the steel industry's survival owes itself to two special factors:

—The steel industry supplies a relatively unchanging market. It can afford to plod to decisions, whereas more consumer-oriented companies live in a world of the quick and the dead. Siemon, for one, also contended that steel industry managers are afraid to speak publicly about their labor problems because they depend on the unions for their jobs.

—The unions have been on their best behavior in the steel industry for the last quarter century because they wanted to see Mitbestimmung extended throughout the economy. Now that their goal has been fulfilled in part, the unions will turn more radical. More generally, it is argued that a legal system of labor relations must not depend for its success on the good will of the unions because this could change in coming years, no matter how satisfactory relations have been in the past.

Another argument is that Mitbestimmung will scare away foreign direct investment in Germany. The case of American objections to the original Mitbestimmung bill is cited. "Capital is shy as a deer," commented Siemon.

Conversely, opponents worry that Mitbestimmung will hamper German industry's efforts to expand abroad in coming years. West Germany, which has been termed an "export giant and foreign investment midget," must spend more on overseas plants if it is to remain competitive internationally.

Workers will resist this process, fearing the loss of domestic jobs, it is asserted. The difficulties of Volkswagen in obtaining union approval for its U.S. project are cited as evidence of this resistance.

German managers worry about where it will all end. The unions and the Social Democratic Party already are committed to pushing for full-parity Mitbestimmung throughout Germany, and managers wonder what would lie beyond full parity. I.G. Metall's Pfromm sees parity as the final goal. "We don't have any thoughts of going further," he said. "We aren't in a position to direct the economy. The Communists say we've been wrong to say we'll stop at parity. But we don't want it all."

Such protestations don't convince everyone. Dr. Walther of the industry federation cited elements within the Social Democratic Party that want to establish total worker control, on the Yugoslav model.

The arguments that have raged back and forth through the postwar decades will no doubt continue. There are no final answers yet, but a look at how the Mitbestimmung game has been played until now can shed light on the subject.

Milestones in the history of Mitbestimmung in Germany

1835: Robert von Mohl, liberal law professor in Tübingen and Heidelberg, proposes joint negotiations between employers and worker groups to improve working conditions.

1848: Frankfurt Constitutional Assembly debates proposal to establish factory committees that could participate in company decision-making. The proposal is unsuccessful.

1905: Prussian Mining Law establishes worker committees in mining firms with more than 100 employes.

1916: Fatherland Auxiliary Service Law decrees formation of jobholder committees in war-related plants with more than 50 employes.

1920: Works Councils Act establishes worker representative units in facilities with more than 19 workers. Units had participation and co-determination rights.

1922: Legislation is enacted requiring companies with a supervisory board to give one or two seats on the board to members of the works council.

1934: Nazis put an end to meaningful works councils and worker membership on supervisory boards.

1946: Allied Control Law No. 22 provides legal framework for rebuilding of works councils.

1947: Ruhr steel companies begin agreeing to parity representation for workers on supervisory boards.

1951: Coal and steel industry Mitbestimmung is legally established.

1952: Works councils are established under German law, and one-third supervisory board participation is introduced for workers outside the coal and steel industries.
1955: Legislation is adopted giving public-sector employes certain participation rights through personnel councils.
1956: Coal and steel industry Mitbestimmung is extended to holding companies primarily engaged in coal and steel.
1972: Strengthened Works Constitution [Council] Act is passed.
1974: New law on participation for public-sector workers goes into effect.
1974: Cabinet approves draft of new Mitbestimmung bill to cover 600 to 650 major companies outside the coal and steel industries. The bill is found to need revision.
1975: Revised bill wins approval of governing coalition.
1976: Revised bill wins parliamentary approval and goes into effect on July 1.

Chapter 2
On-the-Job Experience

Peter Frerk, personnel director of Volkswagenwerk AG, is a strong advocate of Mitbestimmung but acknowledges freely that "we have a mixture [of labor and management] that many people think is impossible."

Mitbestimmung is difficult to conceive for foreign businessmen and trade unionists who think in terms of the traditional adversary relationship between workers and management.

In particular, West German coal and steel industry Mitbestimmung—prescribing labor-capital parity on supervisory boards as well as a management personnel director who enjoys the trust of the unions—may appear unlikely, ponderous and incestuous. If one were to ignore the 25-year history of this industry's labor-capital co-determination, it would be possible to make a case for its being impossible.

Such an argument might go like this:

> Capital seeks maximum revenue and minimum expenses for businesses and industrial enterprises in which it invests. It favors dividends that are as large as consistent with the basic health of the company. Management essentially is the agent of capital and takes a similar point of view. To hold down expenses and remain competitive enough to sell goods, capital pays workers as little as possible. It moves facilities to low-wage areas. It innovates incessantly in order to reduce the number of workers involved in the production process. It must be ruthless in pruning unprofitable operations and lazy or unfit workers.
>
> Labor, on the other hand, seeks the maximum return for the minimum amount of work. Labor resists changes in routine and living location. Workers, having no understanding of the role of profit in commercial and industrial life, don't take kindly to being fired in order to boost earnings for the company.

This inherent opposition of interests must be resolved for the ultimate good of both sides by a corporate system that gives management the balance of power. Management must have sole access to corporate secrets, absolute power to hire and fire, and sovereign authority to plan investments and retrenchments. Labor's only counter-weapon should be the power to strike, which will be used sparingly because strikes cost workers and unions a lot of money.

If you replace capital's preponderance of power by capital-labor equality, you invite chaos. Labor will bring the whole corporate machine to a halt as it seeks and sometimes gets such things as: higher wages than the company can afford, a share of funds destined for dividends, retention of unprofitable operations to keep jobs, and the channeling of investment funds into high-wage areas.

In such a situation, both capital and labor will suffer as companies lose their competitive edge, drop sales and finally go under. Executives, partly dependent on labor for their jobs, will curry favor with workers by avoiding hard decisions.

To install a "neutral man" to break supervisory board deadlocks might prevent the company from being paralyzed by indecision, but in the long run it is equivalent to making corporate decisions by a flip of the coin.

Capital must maintain the upper hand for the good of everyone. The alternative is industrial ruin.

Even in this overstated form, the argument makes some sense. Why then hasn't the German steel industry been ruined by Mitbestimmung? Where has the course of actual events deviated from this catastrophic scenario?

An exhaustively researched answer to these questions is provided by the Biedenkopf Report, a document completed in 1970 by a government-appointed commission of nine professors, chaired by Kurt Biedenkopf, then rector of the University of Bochum and later secretary general of the Christian Democratic Union, the conservative political party. The commission personally questioned 54 persons, including capital and labor members of supervisory boards in the coal and steel and other industries; management men and works-council officials. In addition, it evaluated 1,091 questionnaires submitted by individuals involved in the Mitbestimmung process.

The commission's task was to draw general conclusions from a welter of individual and often conflicting statements. In carrying out this task, the commission subordinated the exceptional, dissenting voice to discern a common pattern. The commission finally recommended an extension of Mitbestimmung but in a weaker form than the montan industry's version.

A second major source of official information on the Mitbestimmung system is the printed transcripts of the four Bundestag public hearings held on Mitbestimmung between Oct. 16 and Dec. 19, 1974. Executives, capitalists, unionists, workers and experts all went on record in a lively and exhaustive public discussion of the government's first draft of the new Mitbestimmung bill. Their voices come through directly and individually, rather than in the summary of a report writer.

Complementing these sources were private conversations with executives and trade unionists and newspaper and magazine articles about boardroom battles that normally are kept quiet under the legal "Schweigepflict" (obligation to silence) that binds board members.

The most general answer to the question why Mitbestimmung hasn't led Germany's steel industry into ruin is easy to infer from the Biedenkopf Report. It is this: The common interest of labor and capital in a healthy company is more important than their differences.

This basic coincidence of interests makes it possible for the two sides to achieve a consensus (albeit sometimes with delays, arguments and horse-trading) on profit creation, dividends, capital investment, closings of unprofitable operations and the choice of company executives.

Profit

The commission found that worker representatives on supervisory boards regarded corporate profit as necessary to making jobs secure and raising wages. Both top managers and capital representatives told the commission that their worker-directors never questioned that profit was the leading principle of corporate activity, although they noted that the existence of worker-directors led to a heavier stress on personnel aspects of decision-making than would otherwise be the case.

Talks with union strategists yield nothing to contradict the Biedenkopf Report fundamentally on this point, though these men believe corporate objectives shouldn't be limited to profit-making. "We see a factory as a social organization, not just a place to make profit," said one I.G. Metall official in explaining why the union pressed for the continued operation of Volkswagenwerk AG's Emden, West Germany, plant even though the plant's current work—production for the U.S. market—eventually will be cut by establishment of a plant in Pennsylvania.

"Profit maximization is conditional," says another I.G. Metall man. "The goals of a modern organization are to keep active, to make sensible products, provide jobs, and to create profit for a minimum return to investors and for new investment. After achievement of an appropriate profit, the remainder should be paid out in wages."

Dividends

The commission found that capital and labor generally were able to reach agreement on dividend payments, though sometimes with difficulty, owing to the workers' preference for reinvestment of profit. This basic labor inclination, motivated by a desire to secure old jobs and create new ones, is tempered, however, by worker recognition that company's dividends must match general market levels if the concern is to be able to tap capital markets.

Evidence of struggles over dividends isn't hard to come by. Mannesmann AG, a major steel and pipe manufacturer, experienced such a battle in 1976, according to a published report that the company won't comment on.[1] The report said worker-directors blocked approval of management's proposed balance sheet on the ground that it didn't make provision for a wage increase later in the year that the workers felt was necessary.

The argument went to the neutral member of the supervisory board for a decision. The neutral man, Ludwig Poullain, management board chairman of Westdeutsche Landesbank Girozentrale, a major state and community-owned bank, voted with capital. The balance sheet—and with it the dividend—was approved.

Ruppert Siemon, of the German Protection Association for Securities Ownership, said he attended the annual meeting in 1976 of a major company outside the coal and steel industry at which a management board member told shareholders he had encountered initial worker-director resistance to the size of a proposed dividend. When Siemon objected that the company shouldn't be influenced by workers in this matter, the management board member agreed but said workers felt that shareholders should have to sacrifice something in view of the fact that some of the staff had been temporarily laid off.

Some companies grant year-end bonuses to workers that are tied to the size of the dividend, Siemon said. In such a case, workers obviously have no interest in a smaller dividend, but management may resist a higher payout because it entails a higher bonus.

The Joint Stock Company Act of 1965 prescribes that if the supervisory board should fail to approve a management-board balance sheet, the matter would go to the shareholders assembly for a final decision. This means that a successful worker-led supervisory board disapproval of a balance sheet ultimately is nothing more than a harassing tactic. Nonetheless, many companies probably would compromise with labor in such a case rather than risk the embarrassment of leaving the drafting of the balance sheet to the shareholders.

Somewhat surprisingly, Mitbestimmung hasn't led to any distortions of wage developments in the coal and steel industry, compared with other industries.

One might expect that union and worker influence in company supervisory boards and management would promote exorbitant wage settlements, but this hasn't been the case. The Biedenkopf commission found there wasn't any essential connection between Mitbestimmung and wage policy. Industrialists also concede this point.

There are two clear reasons for this. First, worker-directors on the supervisory board by and large accept that the board isn't a forum for wage discussions. "The management board is sovereign" in wage matters, said Detlef Hensche, a rather militant trade unionist who formerly served as the labor federation's Mitbestimmung specialist.[2]

Second, the Arbeitsdirektors or personnel directors, on the management boards have a "clear and unambiguous orientation to the employer side" in wage talks, according to Friedrich Kübel, Arbeitsdirektor of Thyssen-Niederrhein AG.[3] This is so despite the fact that the Arbeitsdirektor in most cases is chosen by the unions.

The Biedenkopf Commission conceded that workers often pick up financial information in supervisory board sessions that leads to higher wage demands in good times and lower demands in bad. But the commission noted that similar effects could be observed in other countries that had stricter financial disclosure laws than Germany.

It is normal in West Germany for broad general wage agreements for an industry to be negotiated at a regional level by employers' associations and unions. Wages above the general level then may be worked out on a company-to-company basis through negotiations between the works council and management board. Most employers' associations understandably exclude anyone who isn't independent of the unions. The Iron and Steel Industry Employers Association is an exception in that its leadership includes Arbeitsdirektors from steel companies. Thus, wages in the steel industry are negotiated by the unions on the one side of the table and an association whose leadership includes union-affiliated people on the other.

Despite this appearance of a conflict of interest, no one has complained about wage trends for steel. Even Mannesmann AG's chairman, Egon Overbeck, a declared opponent of the coal and steel industry Mitbestimmung, told the Bundestag hearings that wage negotiations in the steel industry had moved "relatively noiselessly" to agreement in recent years.

Overbeck added a qualification indicating he felt that this was due less to the system than to other factors. He said, "The framework in which we were able to negotiate was determined through the results of previous negotiating rounds in other sectors. No one of us in Germany is in an airless space with regard to his negotiations and agreements. Instead, there is a very definite interdependence, and everyone . . . sets the numbers for those who follow in the negotiation queue. [Because of this] we couldn't move in any significantly different framework in our wage agreements than the trend-setting wage negotiating organizations that preceded us."[4]

Hans-Günther Sohl, chairman of the West German Industry Federation and chairman of supervisory board of the giant August Thyssen Hütte AG steel concern, told the hearings: "*Du lieber Gott*, the profitability of companies in the coal and steel industries has not been endangered by coal and steel industry Mitbestimmung."[5] But he implied that this situation could change.

Wage negotiations in Germany in any case are unusual. The setting of unions' wage demands involves a complex process of consensus-building including public and private discussion among the unions, employers associations, major economic research organizations and the government. The chancellor may even have a quiet word with union chiefs.

The unions often have shown themselves willing to take their cue from these discussions and to orient their demands to expected trends in gross national product and inflation—provided employers do their part by keeping a check on prices. An all-out adversary relationship in wage negotiations between German unions and employers just hasn't existed. Unions, of course, may make big demands at some time in the future to show their independence or because they feel companies are irresponsible in their price policies.

Capital Investment

Worker attitudes toward companies' capital investment range from great enthusiasm to caution, depending on whether or not the investment will create new jobs or reduce existing jobs, the Biedenkopf Commission concluded. Management can count on strong worker support for job-creating investment plans, including help in persuading local governmental bodies to grant necessary permissions. Workers often make direct suggestions for such investment. Some capital representatives who appeared before the commission complained that workers were overzealous about employment-raising capital spending.

When it comes to investments that involve either firing workers or moving them to other locations, worker-directors generally condition their approval on adequate compensation for those affected. Some management-board members told the commission that this attitude made it harder to plan and "sell" investment programs to supervisory boards, but they added that consideration of human aspects of investment generally is considered part of modern management. In fact, companies are specifically required by the Works Constitution Act to reach agreements with their works councils on measures to minimize the adverse impact on workers of major technological changes. But such agreements come after decisions on changes have been made by management and supervisory boards.

There was general agreement, the commission concluded, that workers don't oppose technological change per se. The position of German workers that management may innovate if it is willing to pay workers for resulting job losses and dislocations obviously has some drawbacks from the management point of view. But this attitude is preferable to outright opposition or feather-bedding, examples of which aren't hard to find in other countries.

The commission pointed out, too, that the shifting of social costs involved in technological change isn't particular to Mitbestimmung. "Such a shift can also be agreed in collective bargaining . . . and, as the American example shows, can lead to a considerably higher burden for a company and thus to an indirect limitation on technological progress than has been attributed in the past to institutional Mitbestimmung," the commission said.[6]

The Joint Stock Company Act doesn't designate capital investment as requiring supervisory boards' approval. But company bylaws normally give supervisory boards a veto over investments exceeding a certain size. The shareholders' assembly theoretically has power to overrule this veto by a vote equivalent to three-quarters of ballots cast.

Closings and Layoffs

The most spectacular series of closedowns and reorganization moves that has taken place under Montanmitbestimmung was the consolidation of the German hard-coal industry between

1958 and 1968. The scope and impact of the reorganization—which led to creation of the Ruhrkohle AG group—are suggested by the fact that the number of coal miners in the Ruhr was reduced by 342,000, or 53%, from 1957 to 1968.

Experts disagree about the influence of worker co-determination in this process. Proponents claim the system proved itself during these years; opponents assert that Mitbestimmung played a part in bringing on the crisis.

Ewald Bergk, management board secretary of the I.G. Chemie-Papier-Keramik Union, appearing for the German Trade Union Federation during the 1974 Mitbestimmung hearings, said:

"The authenticity of Mitbestimmung is very clearly proved here, I believe: the reordering of the hard-coal industry could be accomplished not least because of the large influence of the unions, in cooperation with the worker representatives in the supervisory board."[7]

During a 1969 discussion, Ludwig Rosenberg, then chairman of the German Trade Union Federation, said, "The fact that the development in the coal industry went so disturbance-free, let us say almost without difficulty, without doubt must be traced to the introduction of Mitbestimmung. . . . Just the fact that two partners steadily sit down with each other leads simultaneously and unconsciously to a situation in which one draws the interests of the other more or less into his thinking."[8]

But Dr. Walther, head of the industry federation's legal department, claims that equal representation of workers on the boards of coal-industry companies prevented an early recognition of structural problems besetting coal and thus helped create the crisis.

In 1969 Helmut Schmidt, then chairman of the Social Democratic Party's parliamentary group, said that late recognition and difficult solution of the coal-industry crisis resulted from the "general conservative tendency of human thought processes." He said this applied to mine owners, management and workers. "No one can absolve himself," Schmidt said.[9]

The Biedenkopf Commission was very cautious in its assessment of Mitbestimmung's impact on the coal crisis and its solution. It played down the role of co-determination in working out the problem, but concluded that at least Montanmitbestimmung doesn't prevent modernization.

The commission noted that heavy government aid to the coal industry and to laid-off workers meant an easier test for the system than otherwise would have been the case. It said that the industry itself was helped through a host of protectionist measures, including duties and quotas on imports and freight subsidies. In addition, the government made large payouts in connection with the closing of the mines. Funds earmarked for this purpose totaled 1.051 marks in 1968 alone.

(Based on the mark's value of about 25 cents at the beginning of 1968, this was equivalent to payments of almost $262.8 million. Strength of the mark since then has been such that in early 1977 it was holding above 40 cents in foreign-exchange trading.)

The commission went on to remark that "Montanmitbestimmung by no means prevents streamlining of considerable scope." It said the index of coal production per hour worked rose to 143.1 in 1968 from 100 in 1962, and thus outperformed the national industrial average of 142.7. The index for the iron-producing industry also rose to an above-average 145.5.[10]

After investigating the coal industry consolidation and the other cases, the commission summed up, rather vaguely, "It can be determined that Mitbestimmung in the montan industry in certain, by no means seldom but also not too frequent cases, has led to delays of decisions on capacity reductions and closings, but not to final refusal of suggestions and goals of company leadership."[11]

This is faint praise, but at least it rebuts the idea that Mitbestimmung and modernization are completely incompatible. In other countries, capacity reductions and closings often lead to slowdowns, wildcat strikes and worker sit-ins. These costly and unpredictable forms of "industrial action" may well be more inimical in the end to timely adjustments of capacity than is a system that lets workers in on decision-making from the beginning.

The commission noted that the presence of worker-directors on supervisory boards of coal and steel companies led to an "early recognition of personnel consequences" involved in plant closings. It said this was "desirable and is to be expected from Mitbestimmung."

The choice of management-board members is the most important single task of the supervisory board under Mitbestimmung. The equal say of workers in the choice of coal and steel executives in past years raises questions about the type of person chosen for office and how he performs once chosen.

The Biedenkopf Commission found that the joint labor-capital interest in a healthy company meant that worker representatives were as eager to find highly qualified people to fill top-management posts as other directors were. The only difference in outlook was that labor representatives tended to place higher value on "personal conduct" and "leadership capacity" than capital directors did. The commission determined that worker representatives didn't attempt strongly to influence the choice of Vorstand members other than the Arbeitsdirektor. Nonetheless, the commission did detect some signs of growing worker-director interest in other selections.

One such case came up in the Bundestag hearings. Without naming names, Heinz Oskar Vetter, the labor federation chairman, cited a case in which worker and union representatives blocked the election of a montan industry Vorstand member to the post of Vorstand chairman. The incident indicates that workers can form a vital part of the "constituency" of management-board members in the industry.

How much influence do montan workers exert on behavior of Vorstand members? An industry official said, "Some Vorstand members take care to maintain good relations with the unions. Others don't have a particularly good relationship. In general, the unions don't oppose the best man being selected for the job, regardless of his relations with them. They can't take the responsibility for a bad choice."

Nonetheless, conversations with many close observers of the German industrial scene reveal a suspicion that montan industry managers are only too aware of their partial dependency on the unions. Ruppert Siemon of the German Protection Association for Securities Ownership sees these managers as sitting in a sack whose drawstrings are held by the unions. The personnel director of a major company outside the montan field said, "It's hard to get an objective opinion on Mitbestimmung from Vorstand members in the montan industry because they feel dependent on the unions."

He might have added, of course, that management-board

members can't really afford to be candid about their company's capital directors or their bankers, either. But this doesn't alter the fact that the power of worker-directors in the montan industry can make life more difficult for managers simply by enlarging the group whose consent is necessary for management action.

One montan industry executive who is outspoken about the system is Egon Overbeck, the management board chairman of Mannesmann AG, which had the balance-sheet battle. He told the Mitbestimmung hearings that the frequent "compulsion to agree" created by Montanmitbestimmung "by no means leads to sensible decisions." He claimed that the coal and steel system was "not a good model."

Such unguarded pronouncements haven't won appreciation form the worker-directors. Overbeck noted that a worker-director once petitioned the board to "slip a muzzle" on him after he made some outspoken comments at an annual meeting.

Overbeck continued: "That led to a special Aufsichtsrat session. I am sorry I must say these things here. We all have, I believe, certain understandable inhibitions about relating details from our own companies. . . . But I may nevertheless mention this. This question was then handled in very detailed fashion in the Aufsichtsrat. The petition finally was refused because, I believe, the Aufsichtsrat recognized that it hadn't any authority to forbid me to speak when I was talking about tasks that lie within the realm of my responsibility."[12]

Public comments such as Overbeck's are rare. The workers are part of the power structure in the montan industry, and the executives know it. Gone are the days when, as one knowledgeable observer said, the montan industry was run "along paramilitary lines."

Helmut Kater, Arbeitsdirektor of Eisenwerk-Gesellschaft Maximilianshütte mbH, wrote of the new leadership style:

"The management of a company under the Montanmitbestimmung system as a rule can risk conflict with the workers and the works councils only if these conflicts are factually and socially justified. In this way, the number of possible conflicts arising from the arrogance of authority has been reduced to a minimum in this area."[13]

The power of unions in the choice of montan industry executives has led some observers to question whether unions might not try to "blackball" executives who oppose them on specific issues, thereby in effect controlling the job market for executives. Such a development would, of course, strongly inhibit all but the bravest executives from taking antiunion stands.

So long as workers have an equal say with capital on management selection only in the montan industry, executives who run afoul of the unions in that area at least usually have the choice of moving to another industrial sector. But the widening of parity Mitbestimmung throughout the society might raise serious questions about the independence of executives and create the need for specific safeguards.

It was in response to such fears that Vetter mentioned in the Mitbestimmung hearings the case of the executive whose appointment to Vorstand chairmanship was blocked by worker and union representatives. He testified:

"It was asked if, in connection with Mitbestimmung, a Vorstand member's contract isn't renewed, whether this man or woman would again and again run up against resistance in connection with a new position and whether there could thus arise something like an employer's monopoly for the unions. . . .

"I want to cite an example of how nowadays [worker-directors] act in Vorstand questions. It recently became known to me personally that in a montan company a Vorstand member who was up for Vorstand chairman didn't get elected. One might assume now that he would now be up against the general rejection of the unions and the worker representatives. Exactly the opposite was the case.

"In another company there was a need to fill a Vorstand post. In the works council and among the union representatives on the supervisory board there was a quick recognition that this man who wasn't elected as Vorstand chairman in the other company could make an excellent specialist representative in the Vorstand. He was then unanimously elected."

Vetter said that an "employer monopoly for the unions" wasn't possible in practice because "the interest of the worker representatives is precisely in the optimal makeup of the Vorstands. The Vorstands in their central task in the leadership of the company are finally the guarantee for the workers of the company."[14]

The principle, then, is "the best man for the job." But, as the Germans say, "the devil lurks in detail." There can still be disagreement about who is the best man.

What is the atmosphere at the altitude of Aufsichtsrat? The Biedenkopf Commission ascertained quickly that conflicts were rare in formal supervisory board meetings. The commission said it was told "almost stereotypically" that meetings went smoothly and that votes almost always were unanimous.

Investigating this phenomenon, the commission discovered that potential conflicts normally were solved in advance of meetings in informal conversations among worker representatives and between worker-directors and the Vorstand. By the time the meeting rolled around, the Vorstand typically had obtained the consent of the workers for its plans. This tended to limit discussion in the meeting itself and made it easier for the Vorstand to obtain capital's approval—a fact that some shareholder representatives resented.

Pre-meeting caucuses among the worker-directors tend to build unity on the labor side of the supervisory board table and make it difficult for labor to change its position within one supervisory board session, the commission found. The monolithic worker approach also tends to drain Aufsichtsrat meetings of the give-and-take of lively debate.

Management members often take a cue from their preparatory meetings with worker-directors as to what kind of labor response they can expect toward particular proposals. Some management initiatives probably die in embryo without ever reaching capital's ears as a result of these talks, the Biedenkopf Commission said.

In cases where conflict does remain unresolved when the meeting starts or where it breaks out at the meeting, the matter still isn't likely to come to a vote. There is reluctance on both sides of the board to leave the final decision in a disputed case to the designated "neutral man." The result is that decisions are delayed while compromises are made and bargains struck.

Thus, the rarity of disputed votes doesn't mean there aren't any disputes. It means these disputes usually are solved prior to voting. This is the "compulsion to agree" to which Mannesmann's Chairman Overbeck referred, rather disparagingly, at the Bundestag hearings.

Whether or not there is any such compulsion, agreement may be less of a sure thing than in the past. Hans-Günther Sohl, president of the West German Industry Federation, who had experience with Montanmitbestimmung as management-board chairman and later as supervisory-board chairman of August Thyssen-Hütte AG, said during the 1974 hearings:

"To my knowledge, the number of disputed votes that have taken place in the supervisory boards of montan-industry companies has been greater since 1970 than the number of disputed votes in the previous years, that is from 1953 until 1970."

Sohl attributed the increase to "periods of bad [economic] weather" that put a strain on the capital-labor relationship. He pointed out, in addition, that even if cooperation between labor and management in the montan industry had been good on the whole in the past, it couldn't be assumed that this would last indefinitely into the future. New legislation, enduring for many years, shouldn't be based on previously good personal relationships between labor and management, he said. Times can change.[15]

The severest critics of Montanmitbestimmung complain of the hurdles that the capital side has had to cross to obtain the agreement of workers. Gottfried Walther of the West German Industry Federation said flatly, "You don't get any important business through in the montan industry without logrolling." He gave what he called a typical example.

Some years ago, he said, a montan industry company sought to name a well-qualified man to its Vorstand. Worker-directors said they had nothing against the man, but they nevertheless conditioned their necessary endorsement upon the company's meeting of several demands. Key demands that the Arbeitsdirektor be given responsibility for the company newspaper and the building department eventually were met. A demand that the Arbeitsdirektor determine who is to be promoted to managerial white-collar positions was refused. The Vorstand candidate then was endorsed by the worker-directors.

Walther said, "The effects of having a union man as head of the company newspaper can scarcely be overestimated. Soon all the staff members share the union point of view."

He continued, "You wonder what the building department has to do with the unions? It formerly was customary for companies to provide housing for Vorstand members. If the wife of a Vorstand member complained to her husband that the house needed painting, he would either have to suffer a marital argument or go to the Arbeitsdirektor as head of the building department and ask for a painter. The Arbeitsdirektor would, of course, say, 'Yes, but what can you do for me?' "

The story illustrates that worker powers under the Montanmitbestimmung system aren't limited to co-determining matters that are listed in the formal catalogue of Aufsichtsrat duties. Through imaginative bargaining, workers can transform the power to approve a Vorstand appointment into such things as control over the company newspaper and executive housing—areas that lie completely outside the supervisory board's purview.

The Biedenkopf Commission found that workers often conditioned their approval of various company plans on adequate consideration of the social aspects of the plans. In cases of mergers, workers often insisted that these be structured in such a way as to prevent a loss of their Mitbestimmung rights. The latter demand often led to "the establishment of boards similar to Aufsichtsrats and to the acceptance of two Arbeitsdirektors in the Vorstand of the new company."

However, the commission also said it saw only limited evidence that worker-directors coupled their approval of certain company decisions with demands that were completely unrelated to these decisions—a category into which the incident related by Walther undoubtedly would fall.

The heavy influence of the unions in Montanmitbestimmung on the whole has been positive, the Biedenkopf commission found. The union representatives on the board tend to have a wider viewpoint that offsets the narrower "plant-egoism" of the internal worker-directors.

Union men claim that worker-directors from within the company tend to see corporate planning in too narrow a context and to ignore the bigger picture of how planning relates to industrywide problems and to national economic policy. The commission learned, for example, that external union representatives played an important role in the reconcentration of the steel industry in the 1960s, counteracting the "strongly company-based behavior of worker-directors from within the company."

Unions can amass impressive expertise for the worker side of the board, as shown by the case of Fried. Krupp Hüttenwerke AG. Gerhard Leminsky, an official of the German Economic and Social Institute of the DGB and a member of the supervisory board at Krupp Hüttenwerke, described the worker side of Krupp's board this way:

The 10-member labor side breaks down into four internal-company representatives and six outsiders named by the unions. The six outsiders are Leminsky; Rudolf Judith, the I.G. Metall union official responsible for Mitbestimmung in the iron and steel industry; W. Thönnessen, deputy general secretary of the International Metal Workers Union Federation in Geneva; Adolf Mirkes, chairman of the leather workers union; H. J. Knieps, management-board member of the union-owned Bank für Gemeinwirtschaft, and N. Scheffler, former mayor of Hohenlimburg, where Krupp has a plant, and now a member of the Bundestag.

Leminsky said Judith acts as spokesman for the group. Thönnessen has expertise on such international matters as multinational companies, raw-materials supply, international division of labor and foreign currency. Scheffler concerns himself primarily with the regional impact of investments. Knieps specializes in finance policy. And Mirkes has wide experience in an "economic area that has been hit hard by structural adjustments." Leminsky himself takes particular interest in economic aspects of company policy, humanization of work, personnel planning and the social-policy aspects of Mitbestimmung. The four company-internal representatives bring into Aufsichtsrat discussions problems stemming from work within plants.

Leminsky said it would be impossible for central union headquarters to manipulate worker representatives by "tele-guidance," a possibility often brought up by Mitbestimmung opponents.

"Mitbestimmung in a company must serve the employees of the company and secure their jobs over the long term. My task as an outside representative is to contribute to this goal. It is completely impossible to try to pursue a policy in the Aufsichtsrat that places in question the long-term security of jobs."[16]

This is another way of saying that although outside representatives bring the "big picture" to bear on company affairs, they can't impose this picture on a company to that company's detriment. A case in point from outside the montan industry is opposition by I.G. Metall chairman Eugen Loderer to a price rise by Volkswagenwerk AG in 1976.

Loderer, deputy chairman of the VW supervisory board, opposed the increase on the ground that it was inflationary, but he couldn't gain the support of worker representatives on the board, who felt the long-suffering company needed cash, a union source said.

The neutral man of Montanmitbestimmung is the natural whipping boy of those management figures and shareholders who oppose the system. To management, he is an uncertainty. To capital, he is a symbol of its inability to ensure that its will is done on the supervisory board.

Their opposition is to be expected. But the Biedenkopf Commission, whose findings generally were favorable to the Montanmitbestimmung system, also rejected the institution of the neutral man. A commission survey found that in 72% of the organizations it polled, the neutral man didn't cast a deciding vote even once from 1964 to 1968. The commission hearings showed that the neutral man felt overburdened in conflict situations, reluctant to cast the deciding vote. For a neutral man to vote to break a tie, he must assume responsibility for a decision about which he may have little or no specialized knowledge.

The neutral man, as noted, normally is nominated by the worker side, while the capital side names the chairman. One union man, asked to describe an average neutral man, said, "He may be a local politician, a judge, a state politician. In general, he is an SPD [Social Democratic Party] man."

Noting the neutral man's problems, industry federation's Walther said, "Suppose he is a minister or teacher who can't even imagine the 200 million marks involved in an investment decision. He is overchallenged in the job. He doesn't take part in a vote. He makes a telephone call or goes to the bathroom. Then the two sides agree."

In any event, it is safer for each side to compromise than to take a chance on winning the neutral man's vote. The desire of both sides to avoid risks leads to the paucity of contested votes.

This doesn't mean the neutral man is always a useless figurehead. On the contrary, many neutral men see their primary role as that of mediator, seeking to bring both sides together to an agreed joint position. To carry out such a role, the neutral man must enjoy the confidence and respect of both sides.

If the neutral man's position appears difficult, the Arbeitsdirektor's job has a prima facie look of being impossible. To his detractors, the Arbeitsdirektor is a double agent, a man of hopelessly divided loyalties who must develop a schizophrenic mentality in order to survive. He may even be unconstitutional, it is argued.

To boosters, the Arbeitsdirektor is a vital and constructive factor in the Mitbestimmung system of the coal and steel industry, who ensures that company decisions take account of the needs of the workers.

The Arbeitsdirektor, unlike other worker-directors and unlike the neutral man, is a member of the Vorstand, rather than the Aufsichtsrat. He is thus directly involved in the day-to-day operations of the company as the member of top management in charge of personnel.

In coal and steel companies, he may not be chosen against the wishes of the worker side of the Aufsichtsrat. In coal and steel holding companies, he legally may be chosen over the worker side's objections, but in practice he normally isn't. In both types of company, it is usual for the unions actually to name the Arbeitsdirektor. Once chosen, the Arbeitsdirektor becomes a full member of the management board. His problem is to do justice both to his constituency—the unions and workers—and to the company he legally represents.

An apparently successful practitioner in this tricky position is Karl-Heinz Briam, Arbeitsdirektor of Fried. Krupp Hüttenwerke AG. The I.G. Metall union speaks highly of his achievements at Krupp. Briam went to Krupp in 1972 from I.G. Metall, where he had worked in a journalistic capacity, using previous experience in newspapers, radio and TV.

He bridled at any suggestion that his job at Krupp may be schizophrenic. "I am with the employer," he said. "I'm the opponent of the unions—if you want to use that word—if there's a conflict." He said every company must have a personnel director. "What is better? To have a director who is the enemy of the worker or one who enjoys their trust? This doesn't mean he does everything they want."

He said that during a heat wave he rejected a worker request for extra pay to compensate for the heat. He said he told the petitioners: "I'm sorry, I can't banish the heat with more money."

Briam said he sees his job as drawing the human aspect into all phases of corporate decision-making. During the 1975 steel crisis, Krupp output was cut 25%, but no one was fired. Krupp dealt with the problem by reducing overtime, cutting work to subcontractors, holding special training classes during work hours, and transferring workers from one plant to another.

Other methods employed to keep from firing workers included early pensioning of workers 59 years of age and putting some workers on short hours. The latter were arranged so that no one would lose more than 60 marks (about $25) a month in pay. Briam said these arrangements were "typical of the montan industry." He added that they weren't just a response to the "human problem" created by the steel industry problems but also reflected what he called "economic clear thinking."

He reasoned, "If you fire people, you destroy teams that can't be put back together when the market improves. . . . It costs 70,000 marks [over $29,000] to train a lathe operator. If this man leaves for another company, I can't get him back."

He said that to have fired workers would have hurt the image of the company with the most able young workers, who then would have departed for other concerns. Subsequent retraining would have been expensive. He convinced the Aufsichtsrat that his way of dealing with the crisis was best by saying:

"We want a company that is so strong that every man and woman worker is safe, even in bad times. We want a company with social responsibility and a reputation for a clear-thinking management."

His plan was backed unanimously by the board, he said.

Briam said he didn't feel isolated in the seven-man Krupp Vorstand. There are very few decisions that aren't unanimous on the management board, and the vote never goes six-to-one against him, he said. He remarked that at the time of the interview he was paired with management-board Chairman Robert Mintrop on a particular point, with the others ranged against them.

As Arbeitsdirektor, Briam is deeply involved in making

Krupp's recommendations to the Iron and Steel Employers Association for strategy in yearly wage talks. He also helps out the finance director in investment planning by furnishing long-range wage projections. These projections are "top secret" and never reach the unions, the former union official said.

Briam said he enjoys the confidence of both capital and labor sides of the Aufsichtsrat. His contract as Arbeitsdirektor continues until 1982.

Less happy has been the recent experience of Peter Keller, Arbeitsdirektor of Mannesmann AG since 1961. Keller, a one-time member of the German Embassy staff in Washington and a former union official, was named to the Mannesmann post by Otto Brenner, chairman of the I.G. Metall union until his death in 1972.

Keller's philosophy in the job was that he couldn't become the union's Vorstand agent, although he would strive to form a joint position with the unions on personnel affairs. This arms-length relationship with the unions apparently didn't disturb Brenner but became anathema to Eugen Loderer, Brenner's successor at I.G. Metall, and the vice chairman of the Mannesmann Aufsichtsrat. Around I.G. Metall, Keller became known as a man who had "switched over" to the capital side in his thinking.

This attitude manifested itself in 1975 during the recession, when Mannesmann, unlike other steel companies, made a large profit on sales of heavy steel pipe, union sources said. Management wanted to close down a 600-worker plant at Kallethal, a rural area with no work opportunities for those to be displaced. I.G. Metall took the position that the plant should be kept open, at least temporarily. Keller argued that the unit was unalterably unprofitable and should be shut.

An I.G. Metall man said later, "It wasn't necessary that he agree with us, but at least he should have seen our side of the argument a bit. Instead, he said publicly he was a manager just like any other." The plant was closed.

Keller's version is somewhat different. "I made a compromise suggestion: instead of closing the whole plant, to keep it open for about 150 people. This was refused by the union as not enough. They played a game of everything or nothing. This, of course, they don't talk about nowadays."

The incident nevertheless was part of the background when

in the first half of 1976 it became known that the unions would oppose Keller's reappointment as Arbeitsdirektor. But despite the wrath of the formidable Eugen Loderer (who helped scuttle Rudolf Leiding's career as management-board chairman at Volkswagenwerk AG), Keller wasn't dumped.

Keller had the support of labor supervisory-board representatives from within the company, who reportedly considered him a fair man despite his acknowledged commitment to the management side. The upshot was a compromise involving Loderer, Mannesmann management-board Chairman Egon Overbeck, and internal-company worker representatives, under which Keller was given a one-year contract instead of the three-year pact sought by management.

The philosophical counterargument to those who claim the post of Arbeitsdirektor is a Janus-faced institution is suggested by Ernst Viebahn, Arbeitsdirektor of Thyssen-Giesserei AG. He wrote, "The role conflicts of the Arbeitsdirektor find their match in the conflicts of other Vorstand members. In particular, the so-called loyalty conflict of the Arbeitsdirektor and workers (unions) has its parallels in tension conditions of other Vorstand members between concerns of the company and those of its (large or small) shareholders.

"To infer an identity of interests between a company and its various groups of shareholders from the interest conflict between the company and its employees is false and short-sighted. These role conflicts—long defined by sociology—are signs of a highly industrialized society and exist in all areas of political, economic and cultural life."[17]

Those who contend the Arbeitsdirektor may be unconstitutional base their argument on article nine, paragraph three of the German Constitution, which guarantees the "right to form associations to safeguard and improve working and economic conditions. It is contended that this right is injured unless unions and employers are completely independent of each other in collective bargaining, a condition that obviously isn't met institutionally when Arbeitsdirektors selected by the unions sit on the employers' wage-bargaining unit.

Similar objections might arise if, for example, the worker side of the Aufsichtsrat forced the management to make special provisions for meeting anticipated special wage demands, as they attempted to do at Mannesman AG.

The issue has never been decided by the German Constitutional Court at Karlsruhe.

The full-parity Mitbestimmung of the coal and steel industries has been paralleled in other sectors since 1952 by one-third worker participation on supervisory boards in companies with 500 or more workers.

By and large, the system of one-third board participation by workers in other industries proved popular with industrialists and unpopular with unions. The system is of largely historical interest now because it has given way in companies with more than 2,000 workers to the new near-parity situation. It remains in effect only in those companies with 500 to 2,000 employees.

The system had the merits from the employers' point of view of giving the workers a voice and an ear in top-level decision-making while allowing capital to overrule them with a clear majority in any dispute. Workers were limited to a consultative role, though this role didn't prevent them from casting dissenting votes as a protest against company decisions to which they objected.

The unions played a relatively small part in the one-third system. The Biedenkopf Commission found that when given a choice, workers tended to send men to the Aufsichtsrat from the works council, rather than to bring in outsiders. In 85% of the companies outside of coal and steel surveyed by the commission, no external worker representative sat on the board. In some cases, this undoubtedly was the case because companies purposely kept boards small to exclude unionists; only after the first two seats have been filled from within the company may outsiders be brought in; this automatically excluded union outsiders from boards of six and fewer members.

The low participation of unions tended to reduce the militancy of worker-directors. It also meant that labor representatives had an intimate knowledge of the company they were overseeing.

The Mitbestimmung hearings showed that the system of nominal one-third representation sometimes worked out to less than that in reality. Rudolf Bauer, a worker-director at BASF AG, told the hearing that capital representatives excluded workers from Aufsichtsrat committees and that the Vorstand provided only "very thin" information to the worker side.[18]

Committees can play an important role in Aufsichtsrat activities. The committees do preparatory work for full-board decisions and in some cases act in lieu of the full board. A committee can, for example, act on its own in cases where the Aufsichtsrat decides to designate some particular type of Vorstand business as needing Aufsichtsrat approval; the actual approval may be delegated to a committee.

Georg Badeck, member of the Hoechst AG supervisory board, told the parliamentary hearings that workers were excluded until 1968 from the company's finance committee. He added that at the date of the hearing, workers still hadn't managed to get into the supervisory-board presidium, a small group of shareholder representatives that prepares decisions for the full board.[19]

The Biedenkopf Commission found that in companies it checked outside the montan industry, workers had seats on only half the Aufsichtsrat committees. In the montan industry, virtually every committee had a worker member, and in the majority of cases committees were equally manned by worker and capital representatives.

Volkswagenwerk

If worker-directors at most plants were relatively impotent in terms of company policy under the one-third participation law, they wielded strong powers at Volkswagenwerk AG because of particular circumstances. The supervisory board of the auto producer consisted under the old law of 21 members, of whom seven represented labor. However, four of the 14 capital representatives came from the federal government in Bonn and the State of Lower Saxony, each of which owns 20% of Volkswagen, and each of which must consider factors other than maximization of profit. A fifth was Walter Hesselbach, then chairman of the management board of union-owned Bank für Gemeinwirtschaft in Frankfurt. The composition of the capital side gave labor the possibility of forming decisive coalitions in its favor (although Hesselbach is reported to have voted with the capital side).

The power of labor at Volkswagen—obviously increased by the new law—made itself evident most spectacularly in recent years in the resignation of VW chairman Rudolf Leiding in 1974 and in the conditions attached to the establishment of a VW assembly plant at New Stanton, Pa.

Leiding, a hard-nosed production man with little taste for supervisory-board politics, apparently never grasped the significance of worker power at Volkswagen and chose to combat unions instead of using persuasion. Union sources cited his actions in January 1974, just before labor negotiations. (Unlike most German companies, Volkswagen negotiates directly with the union rather than through an employers' association.) Leiding, the union sources said, sent a letter to the homes of all VW workers, asking for restraint in the wage talks. The sources claimed that the letter was intended to reach the workers' wives, in the hope they would try to restrain the militancy of their husbands.

Whatever the motive, the letter infuriated I.G. Metall's Chairman Loderer, deputy chairman of the VW supervisory board, and hardened union opinion against Leiding, union sources said. An arbitrated settlement led to a large wage increase, amounting to 11% in a 10-month period in 1974 and 13% in a 14-month period through January 1975. (Presumably, Loderer was infuriated in his capacity as I.G. Metall chairman because as a supervisory-board member, he isn't supposed to concern himself with wage matters if the freedom-of-association article of the German Constitution isn't to suffer).

The poor personal relationship between Loderer and Leiding already had poisoned the atmosphere when Leiding announced in May 1974 that he favored the establishment of a manufacturing facility in the United States to cut freight costs and avoid problems associated with the rising value of the mark.

The proposal ran into resistance from I.G. Metall and the State of Lower Saxony, which worried about the impact on jobs of such a plant, and from Volkswagenwerk AG finance director Dr. Friedrich Thomee, who contended VW couldn't finance the project. Leiding and Thomee feuded over the issue as the year wore on at a time when the company had to cope with the auto-market recession caused by the sudden spurt in oil prices in late 1973 and early 1974.

In November 1974, the supervisory-board chairman, Josef Rust, stepped down, in part because he was unable to restore peace in the company. Leiding himself resigned in December.

Later, it was announced that VW had sustained a 1974 loss of 807 million marks. Leiding's position at VW no doubt was weakened by the severity of the losses. But there is little question that the antagonism of the union helped push him out of office.

One VW source said following the event, "Leiding perhaps still would be VW's chief if he'd stayed out of union affairs. You don't have to fight every fight. True, sometimes you have to fight, to break down the door. But sometimes you just have to knock and it opens."

Alfred L. Thimm, director of the Institute of Administration and Management at Union College and University, concluded about the Leiding affair:

"If we consider the VW experience . . . as a preview of managerial behavior under 'equal co-determination,' we can . . . anticipate that top managers will be assessed as much by their ability to get along with the union as by their entrepreneurial qualities."[20]

Indeed, a realization of the importance of good union relations appears to have led to the appointment of the Rheinstahl AG management-board chairman Toni Schmücker as Leiding's successor early in 1975. As the man who streamlined and sold off Rheinstahl to August Thyssen-Hütte AG in 1973-1974, Schmücker earned a reputation as a man who knew how to deal with workers during difficult times in a montan-industry company.

Said Loderer of the union after the appointment, "Toni Schmücker has long experience with co-determination and knows how to build our understanding into his plans. He also knows he can't operate against us for long."[21]

The second major demonstration of worker strength at VW came in April 1976 when the supervisory board unanimously approved a long-discussed project to establish the plant in the United States to assemble Rabbit-model cars. Shortly after the decision, I.G. Metall quickly let it be known that worker-director approval had been given only on several conditions.

The union said Aufsichtsrat approval would be required for any increase in the amount of U.S. content of the American-assembled cars or any change in German employment planning resulting from the U.S. project. It said these stipulations were legally justified by Article 111 of the Joint Stock Company Act allowing the supervisory board to designate various types of Vorstand business as requiring its approval.

The union conceded that the Vorstand did have one "out" in the event that the supervisory board refused its approval; the Vorstand could appeal to the shareholder assembly, which then could overrule the supervisory board with a three-quarter majority of votes cast. The union said this was a shareholder right that it had long sought to have dismantled. Meanwhile, it noted that workers would react unfavorably to any attempt to call a special shareholders assembly, and thus it was unlikely that Schmücker would try to use this approach.

I.G. Metall union said also that Schmücker had written a letter to Loderer promising not to export U.S.-assembled VW's to Germany.[22] In addition, VW pledged 40 million marks to retool the Emden plant, up to then producing Rabbit-model cars for the U.S. market, so that it could remain in operation following its loss of the U.S. Rabbit business.

Formally, under VW's bylaws, the U.S. project required a two-thirds vote of approval from the Aufsichtsrat, a majority that might have been obtained without worker approval. But a VW insider said it was deemed important to obtain unanimous backing for the U.S. project in order to wipe out any bad feeling resulting from an earlier "split vote" on the board.

Aside from illustrating the power of workers at VW, this case also probably foreshadows future difficulties facing German companies wanting to expand overseas. The union in this case allowed VW its investment abroad, considered vital by the company to maintaining its U.S. market, but exacted a high price in terms of managerial and shareholder prerogatives.

Pfromm of I.G. Metall, discussing future foreign investment in general, said: "There is potential conflict here. That is clear. We say overseas investment is reasonable only if the economic situation in our country is better with it than without it and if our employment isn't affected. We don't back any management that says it's all the same where in the world we invest. It is decisive that some profits go back to our country to be divided up between capital and labor."

Pfromm said Schmücker had been asked about the return of U.S. profits to Germany but he countered by protesting that his

American investment was being made only to maintain the U.S. market rather than to reap profits.

High-level politics of supervisory-board Mitbestimmung is accompanied steadily by the more humble but probably equally important co-determination at plant and office level through works councils.

It would be a mistake to conceive of board-level and plant-level Mitbestimmung as being separate. Normally, worker-directors of the supervisory board are members and officers of the works council.

This duality of roles means that the same worker representative can attack a problem both at the plant and board level. A works council chairman who fails to get action from management at the shop-floor level on complaints about working conditions along a particular assembly line may take the case higher. In his capacity as a worker-director on the supervisory board, he is likely to demand that the finance director report to the board on investments for the "humanizing of work."

The unions are also part of this process. In most cases, a works-council chairman belonging to the supervisory board is also a union member, trained in union schools for his tasks on the council and board. The union stands ready to advise him at all times.

Thus, works councils, worker-directors and unions form a triumvirate representing labor. This combination of forces has led some German businessmen to complain that labor-capital parity on the supervisory board would amount to "overparity" in labor's favor in the company as a whole.

I.G. Metall's Dr. Pfromm sees strong board representation as a necessary complement of works-council activity, however.

"The works council comes in on things a little too late—when the decision has been made," he said. "For example, suppose a works council wants job enrichment in a plant under construction. Management replies that the structure of a new plant already has been set, and this structure doesn't allow job enrichment."

Early consultation at the supervisory-board level with worker representatives on new investments can force management to take worker interests into consideration from the beginning, Pfromm said.

Chapter 3
The New Law

The attitudes and strategies of labor and capital will probably be as important as the formal rules of the game in determining how Mitbestimmung functions under the 1976 law.

The law, though detailed and generally clear-cut, provides only a framework within which workers, management and shareholders are to interact. The measure, for example, cannot regulate the degree of militancy of union representatives, the combativeness of the Aufsichtsrat chairman, the voting behavior of the representative of the leitenden Angestellten, and the relationship of the Arbeitsdirektor to the unions.

Nor can it be predicted whether companies will attempt to evade or soften what they consider unpleasant features of the new law, or in what areas Labor will concentrate its increased powers.

Although the new law is fully effective as of July 1, 1978, clear answers to such questions may be much longer in coming. In the meantime, informed speculation about the future of Mitbestimmung is possible. (The 1976 law applies somewhat differently to various corporate forms, but this chapter generally will deal with the joint stock company, known as the Aktiengesellschaft, or AG. This form of incorporation covers most of the companies embraced by the law.)

Perhaps the most crucial worry of employers is the potentially disruptive effect of increased union representation on supervisory boards. The 1976 law's provision that union-nominated representatives be given two seats on boards of 12 and 16 members and three seats on 20-member boards means that union representatives will have between one-quarter and one-third of the labor seats.

Under the old, one-third rules of Mitbestimmung, although workers were permitted to name outside trade union representatives to board posts, only a handful of outside men were elected. With outsiders' seats now compulsory, unions will have a much larger voice in boardroom decisions.

German unions expect to hold up to 1,700 board posts on the 600 to 650 companies embraced by the new law. These seats are in addition to those held by jobholder directors who are union members.[1]

Robert Lutz, former management-board chairman of Ford-Werke AG, charged that the union men are "non-democratically elected."[2] There is some justification for this charge; though workers have a choice about which union candidates they elect, they can't bar union outsiders outright from the board in favor of internal-company representatives.

During Bundestag committee work on the new bill, the Christian Democrat-Christian Social Union opposition argued that the measure should merely allow union outsiders to take as many seats as they could win in free elections rather than guarantee them a certain number.

The opposition contended that this would strengthen the "democratic legitimation" of the union representatives and increase the "self-determination" of the workers. The Social Democrats and Free Democrats turned back this suggestion, arguing that in theory it could lead to union men getting either all or none of the board seats. If union men held all seats, that couldn't help the "self-determination" of the workers, the parties contended. Their exclusion, on the other hand, would be unfair to unions, which must be given a voice in shaping company policy because they often are called upon to deal with unpleasant consequences of this policy.[3]

Politically, the issue behind this argument was whether to increase the power of the unions that form an important source of support for the Social Democratic Party. The issue was resolved in favor of the unions.

Talks with employers reveal various fears about the type of unionists who will take places on the new boards. A composite picture of the feared unionist would depict a militant, left-oriented ideologue with no feel for industry generally and no knowledge of or particular warmth toward the company he will oversee.

In a typical comment, a Vorstand member at Dynamit-Nobel AG remarked that one of the company's own worker-directors "understands modernization as self-evident. He is a former tool maker. He knows you must modernize to stay competitive. But union intellectuals tend to think politically." An auto executive commented, "We can live with Mitbestimmung but only if politics isn't introduced on the board by the unions."

A conversation with Pfromm of the I.G. Metall union produced little balm for these fears. He commented, "The internal representatives aren't pretrained. They're not so politically aware as the union people. The internal representatives can be misled by arguments that are based on purely local considerations. The union men will be spokesmen for the workers. They will have more courage and a wider point of view."

Though the new law would appear to allow the unions to nominate anyone, including a company worker, to the board, there is little chance that insiders will be chosen. Pfromm says the I.G. Metall union representatives will be drawn from within the union organization at the headquarters and field-office level. These people will be trained by I.G. Metall itself, which has a staff of 75 teachers.

The labor federation tries to ensure that candidates for boardroom seats on the labor side are idealistically rather than financially motivated. The federation insists they donate 12% to 15% of their board salaries to the union-supported Mitbestimmung Foundation, noted Volker Jung, the federation's Mitbestimmung specialist. Pfromm of I.G. Metall said, "We would like to see no pay at all because pay attracts people for the wrong reasons." Gross pay for board members can go as high as 25,000 marks, or $10,425, a year per seat, Pfromm said.

Businessmen also worry that participation of the unions in many fields will lead to the growth of a cartel-like mentality and that union men won't keep company secrets under their hats.

Robert Lutz of Ford-Werke went so far as to charge that union participation on the scale prescribed by the law would be disallowed in the United States on antitrust grounds. German businessmen, he said, were talking of a "totale Verfilzung"—meaning a felt-like interweaving of union directorships.

I.G. Metall, however, allows its officials to serve on only two boards at a time, though the Joint Stock Company Act of 1965 allows a maximum of 10 seats to any one person and though shareholders' representatives frequently sit on more than two boards. The I.G. Metall rule isn't universal, however. Adolf Schmidt, chairman of the I.G. Bergbau (mining) union, at one point held five Aufsichtsrat posts.

Secrecy

The exact limits of secrecy as they apply to worker representatives on the boards are in dispute, though a general secrecy obligation is set out in the Joint Stock Company Act. Hans-Christoph Leo, chief attorney for Esso AG, has written that shareholder and worker directors alike are bound to treat as confidential any information whose disclosure would harm the company. A majority of the Aufsichtsrat may vote to request confidential handling of any particular matter, provided confidentiality is necessary in the company's interest, he said.[4]

The labor federation's Mitbestimmung Foundation contended that each member of the board must decide for himself what must be kept secret in the interests of the company. The majority of the board isn't empowered to muzzle the others, it held. The foundation argued that worker representatives are free under the law to seek outside advice and to make disclosures of board activities insofar as these are necessary to squelch rumors, avoid misunderstandings and prevent unrest.

It conceded that the law doesn't allow disclosure of voting by individual board members or comments made during board meetings that obviously were intended for only those present. But it argued that worker representatives should be exempted from this provision because of their need to inform their constituencies and their need to display their voting record.[5]

One union source confirmed that the unions would "like to see the secrecy obligation more liberally interpreted" but conceded "we're not sure the courts would uphold us." Horst Bergemann, personnel manager of Ford-Werke AG, asserts that the unions would fail in any legal challenge of the secrecy obligation.

Whatever law and the courts may say, Aufsichtsrat sessions aren't always treated as totally secret by participants, and word sometimes leaks into public print about boardroom battles. But the secrecy obligation does act to inhibit the flow of such information and to prevent most board battles from becoming public knowledge.

White-Collar Representative

The leitende Angestellte member of the supervisory board is a major unknown in the new equation. This employee is, in Horst Bergemann's words, "structurally part of management." But he sits on the worker side of the boardroom table.

Is this a formula for creation of a new identity crisis within the system? Will the leitende Angestellte man end up in a position similar to the Hamlet-like neutral man of the Montanmitbestimmung system or its "schizoid" Arbeitsdirektor?

Certainly, the man will face strong pressures, at least in the initial phase of the new Mitbestimmung. Capital will look to him to follow the shareholder line. If he does so, votes on controversial issues theoretically can always be resolved in capital's favor; on a 20-man board the vote would be 11 to nine. The chairman would thus be spared the unpleasant task of using his extra vote to break a tie.

But labor also will be watching closely to see whether the leitende Angestellte representative turns out to be a legally installed Judas. Any leitende who consistently votes with Capital will have to be able to stand a lot of heat.

The leitenden Angestellten generally are defined by German law as employees who have independent power to hire and fire, authority to represent the company or sign documents for it, or duties that require special experience and knowledge. They may not belong to the works council.

The leitende Angestellte is a manager who has reached at least the middle rung of the ladder but is still below the top rung—which is Vorstand membership. The Mitbestimmung law eliminates from membership in the Aufsichtsrat those top-level leitenden Angestellten who report directly to the Vorstand and are empowered to act for the Vorstand in all matters. Vorstand members and the highest-ranking leitenden Angestellten may not sit on the supervisory board on the theory that no man should supervise himself.

The idea of guaranteeing places on supervisory boards for

middle management employees came from the Free Democratic Party, which draws important support from this class. The theoretical justification for this feature, according to Wolfgang Mischnick, chairman of the Free Democrats' parliamentary group, is this: the montan and one-third of Mitbestimmung used a confrontation-prone "two-factor" model involving labor and capital.

The Free Democrats, Mischnick declared, replaced the two-factor model with a three-factor system, combining the elements of labor, capital and upper-middle management. The three-factor model promotes more cooperation and a better balancing of interests among the groups forming the company, Mischnick contended.[6]

This remains to be seen. The unions are highly skeptical of the leitende Angestellte. I.G. Metall's Hans-Adam Pfromm said, "We won't make a prognosis on the voting behavior of the leitende Angestellte. We will follow his voting conduct statistically over a period and later recommend the elimination of this feature if the leitende Angestellte proves to be a shareholder representative rather than a worker representative."

Pfromm said he saw no conflict between his planned statistical study and the statutory obligation to secrecy binding board members. This obligation was designed to protect commercial information, such as profit and sales figures, and is irrelevant to the collection of voting statistics, he claimed. Pfromm said he suspects that the leitende Angestellte representative will represent capital. The leitende Angestellte representative will take the supervisory-board job in order to boost his salary and to attract the attention of the influential shareholder representatives on the board who have close connections with other companies, Pfromm said.

"A good leitende Angestellte certainly will be hired by another company after his first five-year term," the I.G. Metall union man contended.

The Labor Ministry's Karl Fitting, on the other hand, said the "leitende Angestellte isn't a Judas." By reason of his position in the company, he will tend to vote against capital on certain issues, such as suggestions for wage cuts, layoffs and movements of operations abroad, Fitting said.

Pfromm's statistical study won't be the only union measure

aimed at the leitenden Angestellten as a class. In many companies, for example Ford and Opel, the works councils have sought steadily to narrow the definition of the leitenden Angestellten.

At Opel, for example, late in 1976 management considered 500 of the 34,000-employee Rüsselsheim plant as members of the leitenden Angestellten, while the works council argued the number should be reduced to 150.

One motive of the demand is this: Because the works council represents all workers except the leitenden Angestellten, the narrower the definition of the leitenden Angestellten, the more people are represented by the works council.

There's a second reason for the demand, managers suspect: The works councils are seeking to thin the ranks of the leitenden Angestellten to prepare to demand that separate representation on the supervisory board for the leitenden Angestellten be eliminated as unnecessary in view of the group's small size.

In self-protection, the Union der leitenden Angestellten, an organization representing 40,000 such employees, has proposed that legal status be given to the current de facto "spokesman committees" that represent leitenden Angestellten in their companies. As part of the demand, the ULA asks that the definition of the leitenden Angestellten be sharpened in order to end arguments about who and what they are.

The Board Chairman

The most important figure on the supervisory board, of course, is the chairman. He holds the decisive extra vote. His technique in combining persuasion, compromise and firmness can be crucial for the company he serves.

Although the chairman ideally is chosen by a two-thirds majority of the Aufsichtsrat, it isn't always that simple. If such a margin can't be obtained on the first ballot, labor members of the board elect the vice chairman and shareholder members choose the chairman.

This procedure would appear to guarantee a capital representative as chairman. But even here employers show some anxiety. Hans-Christoph Leo of Esso pointed out that a labor representative could be elected chairman on the first vote of a 12-member board if only two capital members cast their votes for a labor candidate. Such a "defection" would give the worker side eight votes, or two-thirds of the total.[7] On 16-member and 20-member boards, the critical "swing" would be three.

If a labor man were elected, the capital side would be in the minority, raising constitutional questions, he contended. To guarantee the constitutionality of the voting procedure, legislators would have had to make clear that only a capital representative could be named chairman. But they "did not have the courage to make this clear in the law," he said.

However, shareholder representatives probably won't be reelected by the general assembly of shareholders unless they're willing to support a capital candidate for chairman. The situation feared by Leo is likely to occur rarely, if at all.

The chairman's main power will be his deciding vote to protect the vital interests of the company as he sees them, but he will strive for as much consensus as possible.

Employers are nearly unanimous in believing that the chairman's decisive vote must be used sparingly. Although capital has the edge over labor on boards, they note, this margin isn't a comfortable one. In the language of U.S. politics, capital doesn't have a strong mandate.

The West German Employers Association said that the basic concept of the law is that the parity composition of the board makes itself felt in the first phase of Aufsichtsrat decision-making. Capital may use its final right of decision only in the second phase, "as a correction to the consequences of parity."

The employers association notes, "The preponderance of capital is burdened by parity. To enforce it presupposes a conflict situation in which both sides confront each other with equal votes, and the formal solution of this conflict contains the danger of actually worsening it."[8]

In other words, the drama of the second vote may intensify bad feelings on the part of labor, with serious consequences for the company at the Betriebsrat, or works council, level. The association believes the chairman must have the courage to use his decisive vote when necessary, but it stresses the need for cooperation on both sides to avoid the situation.

Dr. Walther of the West German Industry Federation made clear that any chairman must think very carefully before using his second vote. "We hope the Aufsichtsrat chairman will use his extra vote, but he is a human being. He can't use it all the time." Suppose, Walther said, that the Aufsichtsrat chairman's full-time job is as a Vorstand member elsewhere and that his contract will come up for renewal shortly. News that he used his second vote will get around and possibly complicate his reappointment.

In addition, Walther said, "He's got to worry about possible strikes and frictions. He must worry about the possibility of unions taking the case to the public."

Robert Lutz of Ford-Werke put it this way: "It will be important not to bull things through by a vote of 10½ to 10 but to achieve a consensus decision by persuasion."

But if consensus is to become the rule and conflict the exception—as it has been in the montan industry— the chairman must be prepared not only to be persuasive but also to make compromises. He very likely will take a straw vote prior to important votes to determine which way the wind is blowing. A negative labor attitude will be the signal for horsetrading.

In the case of proposed major overseas investments that will reduce jobs at home, labor might insist on generous provisions for those who will lose their jobs. It might demand the approval for construction of a domestic plant that could absorb some of those displaced, or it might ask for an unrelated concession—improved cafeteria and medical facilities for the workers, for example.

The chairman will have to weigh the cost of these demands against all the considerations mentioned by Walther. This is the apparent intent of the law.

To be able to use his tie-breaking vote when necessary, the chairman first must be able to ensure that a tie will exist. That is, he must assure himself of unanimity on the shareholder side and make certain that all shareholder representatives cast their votes personally or with valid absentee ballots.

To develop unanimity, the employers association recommends that the capital side of the board should hold caucuses prior to Aufsichtsrat sessions. The association expects labor to do the same, with the union men leading the discussions, as has been the practice in the montan industry. Any maverick capital representatives who vote against capital very often probably won't have their contracts renewed.

The increased importance of shareholder members being present to vote at Aufsichtsrat meetings is likely to cause at least two changes. First, honorary seats aren't likely to be granted to the physically infirm or to persons who live overseas. Second, shareholders will begin choosing alternate members to fill quickly any posts that become vacant.

Shareholder representatives who know in advance that they can't attend meetings will be required to submit absentee ballots giving their vote on all topics on the agenda. The absentee ballot procedure, which also holds for the chairman's second vote, is rather inflexible because it requires the sender to form an opinion prior to Aufsichtsrat discussion and because it doesn't allow the sender to vote on any topics not spelled out on the agenda. The latter disadvantage is likely to result in the demise of the term "miscellaneous business" from Aufsichtsrat agendas, Hans-Christoph Leo indicated.

Conservative lawmakers had urged that the absentee ballot system be replaced by a system allowing the blanket transfer of voting power to another member of the board, but this was rejected in the legislation, primarily on the ground that it would encourage absenteeism.

Neither the absentee ballot nor the proposed voting transfer could solve the problem of so-called accidental majorities arising from the unexpected absence of a capital member, when a member's plane is fogged in, for example.

The law prescribes that the board may make decisions—other than choice of the supervisory-board chairman and selection of Vorstand members—when at least half the members are present. This means that if a capital member is unexpectedly prevented from coming to a meeting, a labor majority would arise.

While the employers have complained loudly about this possibility, it was played down by the majority coalition members of the Bundestag Labor and Social Committee, which helped draft the final bill. The committee in its final report said the majority position was that: "It is not to be feared that accidental majorities [on supervisory boards] will be abusively exploited under this law, which is based on cooperation and not on confrontation."[9]

The industry federation's Dr. Walther wasn't convinced. He conceded that it had been known in the montan industry for union men to abstain from voting when a capital member couldn't show up and hadn't cast an absentee ballot. He contended this was because labor still wanted to demonstrate "that Mitbestimmung had proved itself." Now that the unions have achieved their aim of extending parity Mitbestimmung throughout the economy, "They don't need to prove anything anymore," he claimed.

Karl-Heinz Briam, the former I.G. Metall official who became Arbeitsdirektor at Fried. Krupp Hüttenwerke (a codetermined steel company), scoffed at the idea that unions would exploit accidental majorities. "That would mean the end of cooperation and Mitbestimmung," he said. "Mitbestimmung means cooperation."

Although cooperation may prove to be the rule under the new system, employers are likely to remain uneasy about their slim majorities. In August 1976, the German Protection Association for Securities Ownership began a series of suits in state courts designed to test the constitutionality of the 1976 law. The suits attacked, among other things, the possibilities of "accidental" labor majorities and elections of non-capital chairmen.

The capital members of Aufsichtsrats may also attempt to alter their bylaws to raise the required quorum beyond the legal one-half.

The Personnel Manager

The questions surrounding the leitende Angestellte, union representation and voting strategies all concern the Aufsichtsrat. Uncertainties about the role of the Arbeitsdirektor, or personnel manager, on the other hand, involve the lower half of the two-tier board system, the Vorstand.

The ambiguities surrounding the name Arbeitsdirektor have even caused friction between the Social Democrats and their coalition partners, the Free Democrats. The coalition's original 1974 bill merely specified that one member of the Vorstand should be "predominantly responsible for personnel and social matters." But when the largely watered-down second version appeared, it directed the appointment of an "Arbeitsdirektor."

The friction continued after the compromise was approved on Dec. 9, 1975. The Free Democrats stressed that the Arbeitsdirektor would be chosen as any other Vorstand member. The Social Democrats said the post had been modeled after that embodied in the 1956 Montanmitbestimmung law applying to holding companies in the steel industry.

The 1956 law also provides for an Arbeitsdirektor, but unlike its 1951 predecessor it doesn't give the worker side of the supervisory board the power to veto an unacceptable candidate. Lack of legal veto, however, has meant little in practice; the workers choose the Arbeitsdirektor in the steel holding companies covered by the 1956 law.

The framers of the 1976 law clearly intended to make the Arbeitsdirektor as similar as possible to his existing counterparts in the steel and coal industries. The language of the new law's Article 33, dealing with this post, is largely taken from the 1951 law (and one of the framers of the laws said that the passages in question are written in the same "terrible German").

The similarity of language invites an association of ideas, but legally the Arbeitsdirektor of the 1976 law is quite different from that of the 1951 legislation, because appointments to the post don't legally require the consent of the worker side of the board. Whether the unions in fact control the post will be left to capital and labor to thrash out.

Labor Minister Walter Arendt, a Social Democrat, enunciated his party's conception of the post in a Bundestag speech March 18, 1976, when he said:

> The opportunities for jobholders to influence management policy and other important decisions are supplemented by the provisos regarding the Arbeitsdirektor. In the greater number of the businesses covered by the new law, especially the big ones, I am sure that for the individual jobholder co-determination will be most tangibly embodied by the Arbeitsdirektor. Although his sphere of authority is not laid down by the law, the

> institution itself requires that the Arbeitsdirektor must deal substantially with personnel and social matters.
>
> The interests of management patently demand an Arbeitsdirektor who is accepted by the jobholders and their representatives. Particularly for big business, it can thus be assumed that the Arbeitsdirektor will be a company board member who enjoys a special degree of trust on the part of the jobholders.
>
> Even in the coal and steel [holding] companies, where since 1956 the jobholders have had no power to veto his designation, the Arbeitsdirektor has been appointed at the suggestion of the jobholders' side without a battle of ayes and nays. Why should it be different after passage of the new law?

The political dispute came into the open in the summer of 1976, when Otto Graf Lambsdorff, economic spokesman for the Free Democrats in parliament, charged that the Social Democratic Party was supporting "union attempts to undermine compromises of the [governing] coalition." He said he had learned that two concerns, controlled by the State of Bavaria and the federal government, planned to place union-nominated Arbeitsdirektors on their boards.[10]

The clamor raised by Lambsdorff's protest temporarily halted these plans, but the question of who shall be Arbeitsdirektor remained unanswered for all companies. The law left a lot to be "filled in" by practice in this case.

Employers are expected to resist pressures to give unions the right to name the Arbeitsdirektor. The West German Employers Association contended that union appointment of the Arbeitsdirektor, who is to play an important part in formulation of company wage policy, would undermine the independence of employers and jobholders in wage talks, raising constitutional questions. Any attempt by unions to claim the right to name Arbeitsdirektors should be "uncompromisingly opposed," the association said.[11]

Even those businessmen who abhor the idea of a union-appointed Arbeitsdirektor concede readily they wouldn't want to appoint anyone to the post whom the workers found objectionable because he couldn't function effectively in the job. He might even have to bend over backwards to prove to workers he was being fair. But they insist there is a big difference between capital choosing a director with whom workers can live, and unions being given a formal veto or being allowed to name their own man.

The new law leaves loopholes through which some companies might seek to evade or soften its impact. Whether these will be exploited on any large-scale basis is doubtful because the unions are monitoring company responses very closely.

The biggest apparent loophole is that the law applies only to companies with 2,000 and more workers that have any one of five basic corporate legal forms. Thus, companies have the theoretical possibility of reducing their size or changing their form to escape the law. Because the law applies with differing degrees of severity to the five legal forms, a company could also switch to another form of incorporation.

The five basic forms affected by the law are the joint stock company (Aktiengesellschaft, or AG), company with limited liability (Gesellschaft mit beschränkter Haftung—GmbH), partnership based on shares, (Kommanditgesellschaft auf Aktien—KgaA), companies in the form of a mining Gewerkschaft (Bergrechtlichen Gewerkschaft mit eigener Rechtspersönlichkeit) or profit-oriented economic cooperative (Erwerbs- und Wirtschaftsgenossenschaft).

One of the five, the mining Gewerkschaft, is actually an extinct form. When asked why it was included in the bill, a Labor Ministry expert replied, "As the bureaucrats say, 'It has always been that way.' " The law makes no distinction between privately owned and government-held companies that are in these five forms.

At least one significant addition to this list is the legally mixed form, the GmbH & Co. KG—a partnership in which the general partner is a GmbH usually owned by the limited partners. Generally speaking, a GmbH & Co. KG with more than 2,000 employees will fall under the new law.

To protect basic rights such as freedom of the press, legislators exempted from the law organizations that exist directly and predominantly for purposes of reporting, expression of opinion, politics, charity, education, art, and academic endeavor.

The application of these exemptions may not prove easy.

The magazine publisher Gruner & Jahr AG & Co. has had to contest union arguments that the company is embraced by the law. Gruner & Jahr claimed it clearly was entitled to an exemption, while the I.G. Druck and Papier printers union asserted the firm existed more to make a profit than to serve the exempted purpose set forth in the law.[12]

The variety of company forms that are subject to the law brings differences in the types of Mitbestimmung they get. Justice Minister Hans-Jochen Vogel explained the phenomenon this way:

"[Problems] arise from the fact that the Mitbestimmung law cannot apply to only one legal form but must apply also to various forms in the interests of a balanced inclusion of workers in Mitbestimmung. In the Aktiengesellschaft, the codetermination of the workers is settled in its supervisory board. Other company forms don't necessarily have to have a supervisory board; if such a board is prescribed by the Mitbestimmung law, it doesn't necessarily have the same functions as in an Aktiengesellschaft. The consequence is that there is an unjustifiable Mitbestimmung gap among the individual legal forms. A few legal forms, such as personal companies (Personengesellschaften) and the single proprietorship (Einzel Kaufmann), must be largely left out."[13]

He pleaded for an overall concept to wipe out these differences.

The GmbH illustrates the type of differences to which Vogel referred. Karl Fitting of the Labor Ministry noted that GmbH shareholders are entitled to give orders directly to the management board. If the supervisory board tries to veto an order, the management board can appeal to the shareholder assembly, which then can reaffirm its order, overruling the supervisory board.

Fitting conceded this was a weakness in the law as it applies to the GmbH but said that in practice the shareholder assembly will not choose to "live in permanent confrontation with the worker side of the board." He said it was unlikely any AG would switch to GmbH form to soften the impact of Mitbestimmung, because such a change under German company law would subject a company's voluntary reserves to taxation.

Hans-Adam Pfromm of the I.G. Metall union dismissed the

question as academic because the new law in any case provides capital with the voting edge.

The union has charged that some companies were attempting to escape the law altogether by switching to an ineligible corporate form or by artificially reducing the number of their workers below the 2,000 level. Notable among these, the union said, were:

—An American-owned company that changed its form from GmbH & Co. KG to GmbH & Co. OHG. The OHG (Offene Handelsgesellschaft) is a general partnership in which all partners are unlimitedly liable. It isn't subject to Mitbestimmung under the new law. The GmbH & Co. KG, as noted earlier, in most cases is subject to the law.

—A Swiss-owned German company with 1,700 workers that shifted ownership of its own German subsidiary with 750 employees back to the foreign parent to avoid going over the 2,000 level.

I.G. Metall union and the German Labor Union Federation concede, however, that cases like this aren't numerous. Horst Bergemann of Ford-Werke said some companies will seek to evade the law. But he added, "Any of these maneuvers is dangerous because it might lead to a political situation in which pressures would develop for new changes in the law. The wisest course is to apply the new law exactly under consideration of legal possibilities. The multinationals will be observed very carefully."

Among the hypothetical management ploys to escape the law altogether are: operating a group through a controlling company that either is too *small* to be embraced by the law (i.e. it has less than 2,001 workers), or operating it through a controlling unit that *isn't in a legal form* affected by the law.

The first device is ruled out completely because: If a controlling company is in a legal *form* embraced by the law, the number of its employees for the purposes of the law is the number of employees in the entire group. For example, if a GmbH with 500 workers runs a group of companies having a total of 10,500 workers, the GmbH has an effective work force of 11,000 workers and thus is subject to the law.

The ploy of operating through an exempt corporation would have only limited success because: If a controlling company has a legal form not affected by the law but runs a large group through one or more companies that have forms subject to the law, then the dependent company—with the eligible legal form—that is closest to the controlling unit counts as head of the group and is co-determined. For example, if a controlling KG—an ineligible form—runs a 2,500-worker group through five AG's with 500 workers each, then the AG with the closest relationship to the KG counts as the controlling company. This AG effectively has more than 2,000 workers for the purposes of the law and has a co-determined board under the 1976 law.

In groups embracing several companies, each eligible member corporate body is co-determined, not just the holding company. A simple example would be a group of three AGs, each employing 2,500 workers, in which Company A owns Company B which owns Company C. All three AG companies would have co-determined boards, according to the law.

The shareholder rights accruing to Companies A and B are specially regulated. Under German law the management board of Company A is the shareholders assembly of Company B. The management board of Company B is the shareholders assembly of Company C. However, Article 32 of the new Mitbestimmung legislation places limits on the exercise by management boards of shareholder powers.

Article 32 says that management boards of Companies A and B may make structurally relevant decisions as shareholders only with the approval of the supervisory boards of Companies A and B, respectively. And supervisory board decisions in these matters require a majority of the vote of the *capital side only.* The provision is designed to prevent an accumulation of worker rights in big groups.

Karl Fitting elucidated this principle wryly by saying that the Vorstand of a co-determined company is presumed to be "slightly pink" in the political sense, because it was selected by and is overseen by an Aufsichtsrat in which labor holds half the seats. To ensure that the Vorstand is thoroughly capital-oriented in the exercise of its most important shareholding duties, the law requires the Vorstands to follow instructions of their supervisory boards and leaves the instructions to the shareholders side.

The provision affects decisions on such matters as going out

Main Organs of Large Company Co-determined under New Law

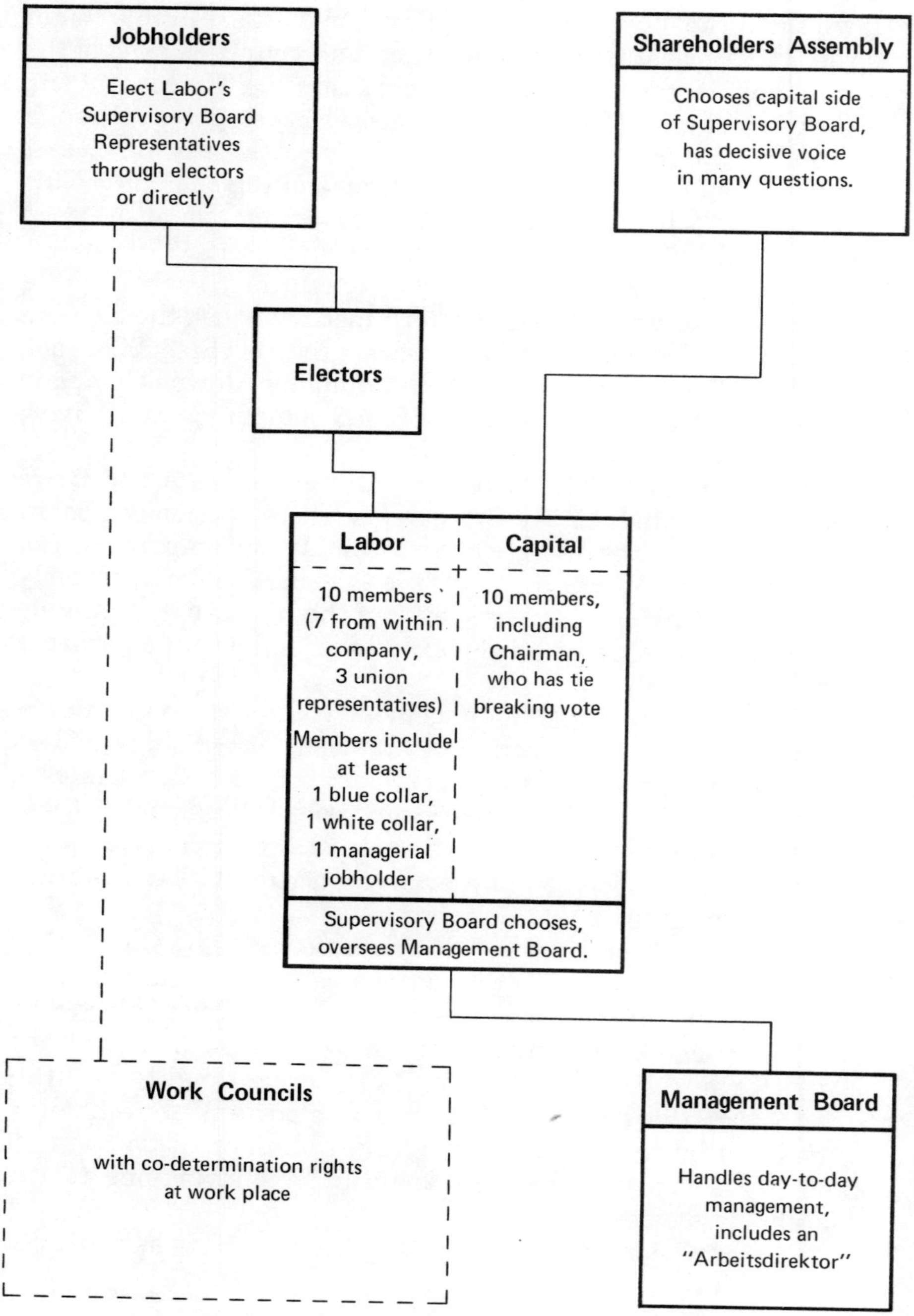

of business, mergers, conclusions of certain types of agreements with other companies and changes of corporate form. It applies only where one co-determined company has a share of at least 25% in another company that comes under the law. (A 25% shareholding gives its owner a veto in the shareholders assembly on certain matters.)

Short of trying to change legal form or reduce the number of its workers, a company might attempt to soften the law by reducing the powers of its supervisory board to the legal minimum—namely the choice and supervision of the management board. This course is hinted at in a booklet of the West German Employers Association that recommends that firms "limit potential conflict" by unburdening the supervisory board of unnecessary chores. It urged a review of company bylaws and rules of business.

Presumably, bylaws might be pruned of requirements that supervisory boards pass upon such business as major investments, bond issues and the acquisition of real estate. "I have urged companies to do this [reduce supervisory board power]," one company adviser said in the summer of 1976. "Some have done it. Now it's too late." The unions now are alert to this possibility and ready to make an issue of it, he said.

Still another evasion technique might be to shift as much supervisory-board power as possible to company committees from which workers are excluded altogether or on which they are given only minority positions. The law specifically guarantees workers an equal number of seats on only one committee—the one that seeks to mediate differences between capital and labor on the choice of Vorstand members.

Though committees were used to weaken worker influence under the one-third Mitbestimmung system, this method is likely to prove less successful in the future. Outside union representatives probably will react strongly to any attempt to isolate them from power centers on the board.

Karl Fitting argued that the law itself implies that workers must be given an equal number of seats on certain committees if they want them. Fitting said a distinction should be made between committees that have the power to make decisions on behalf of the full board and those that only do pre-decision spadework. He held that company supervisory boards shouldn't be allowed to use the chairman's extra vote to set up non-parity committees that have the power to act in lieu of the full board.

His reasoning, which he said is supported by some industrialists, is that the chairman's second vote legally may be used only in single cases. Use of the second vote to give capital an edge in a decision-making committee would "prejudice an indefinite number of future cases," he said. Any unresolvable disagreement in a committee occupied by an equal number of workers and shareholders would have to be resolved by the board chairman, he said.

He didn't see any legal necessity to give workers an equal voice on other committees, although he contended it would be "in the spirit of the law to do so."

The new law prescribes a highly complex election procedure that reflects compromises between the Social Democratic and Free Democratic parties. One German businessman contended that some management boards, overwhelmed by the difficulties of setting up elections under the law's provisions, have adopted "an escapist attitude: 'My name is Hase and I know nothing of these things.' "

The Labor Ministry has estimated that the election process will take from 16 weeks in a company with only one facility to as much as 58 weeks in a far-flung group with a fleet of ships whose crews take part in the balloting.

Outlines of the procedure are contained in Articles 9 to 24 and also Article 34 of the 1976 law (see Appendix), and details are to be filled in by a lengthy set of regulations drafted by the Labor Ministry.

Some major features of the new election procedures:

—Employees have two basic choices on how to select their representatives. First, employees decide whether to vote directly or through electors. Second, they may opt to vote on company-internal candidates as a single group or in two groups—white-collar workers, including the leitenden Angestellten, forming one unit and blue-collar workers comprising the other.

—Nominations of electors and board members always are made by separate action of three groups—the leitenden Angestellten, other white-collar employees and blue-collar workers.

—Union-nominated representatives are chosen jointly, rather than by separate groups.

—Elections of board candidates are decided in most cases according to the principles of proportional representation, allowing minorities to win board seats. Under the system, workers vote for lists of candidates, rather than for individuals, with seats divided among top candidates on each list according to the number of votes received by the list.

—Employees of subsidiary companies take part in elections of the parent company as well as in elections within their own subsidiary.

The law provides that employees may remove their representatives, without needing a specific reason, through a procedure that in most respects parallels the election process. However, a large majority is necessary for a removal. The big majority is required in order to thwart any attempt by constituencies to keep representatives on a short leash—known to lawyers as an "imperative mandate." Any supervisory-board member—capital or labor—may be dismissed by a court for "an important reason" following a petition by a majority of the board. Such a reason might be repeated disclosure of confidential company information, for example.

The voting procedures represent an ornate and ponderous bridge between the electoral concepts of the Social Democrats and Free Democrats. The Social Democrats had favored joint, indirect and majority-vote elections as a means of giving unions maximum influence on the choice of supervisory-board representatives. Their more-conservative coalition partner stressed separate, direct and proportional-representation balloting for the purpose of ensuring maximum "democracy" and protection of minorities.

What the unions and workers do with their new power remains to be seen. The 1976 law obviously gives them enormous power to disrupt and delay company business. But worker-directors have the same duties to the company as the shareholder board members, and they are legally liable in cases where they abuse or neglect their duties (under Articles 93 and 116 of the Joint Stock Company Act).

At the same time, no less an authority than Chancellor Helmut Schmidt has urged workers to take a more activist role in company affairs. At a Social Democratic conference on Mitbestimmung in June 1976, Schmidt urged workers to extend their sphere of board influence beyond matters related to working conditions. "Mitbestimmung doesn't mean just sitting there," he said.

He advised workers to scrutinize carefully company decisions on prices, investment financing, use of profit, mergers and other matters. Chancellor Schmidt said that he had asked workers at several auto companies in 1976 whether they considered it self-evident that the companies should raise prices in response to the then-rising demand. The question provoked puzzlement. He said he was told at one company, "It isn't so self-evident, but this doesn't concern us. It is the Vorstand's business."

Schmidt said that in the case of the financially troubled Volkswagen, he could understand the worker' desire to see more money brought in through higher prices, but he made clear he disapproved of the "let-the-Vorstand-do-it" attitude he encountered in the auto firms.[14]

An I.G. Metall union official said later that Schmidt's remarks had irritated organized labor. He said that in the first place, the capital side of the Aufsichtsrat wouldn't allow price policy to be removed from the sole authority of the Vorstand. He said the union was satisfied with this state of affairs.

"We're a little lucky it's that way," he said. "If we had responsibility for every price increase, that would damage us. The case shows there are limits to Mitbestimmung. The unions don't want to engage that deeply in company policy. This shows Mitbestimmung isn't a first step to Marxist socialism."

This official strikes a moderate note, and his opinion probably represents the majority view. But the unions don't always talk that way. A 1974 labor-federation tract, called "Codetermination Now and No Half-way Measures," began this way:

"The workers and their trade unions want to co-determine, i.e. to break the dominance of capital. With the aid of codetermination, they want to attain the goals the workers are interested in. . . . Why co-determination? Well, there are many reasons—including, unfortunately, some that are the wrong ones. There is, for example, the ideology of the *Social Partnership*. As if the contradictions and clashes of interests of the capitalist economy could be dissolved into peaceful partnership! Deliberately or accidentally, the workers and their trade-unions are alloted a fixed, and usually limited, position in the economy and society under this ideology. This turns into freezing existing conditions. Those who talk of partnership today are going to bat for the ruling classes, though perhaps they do not mean to. Harmony is something for glee clubs, not for the capitalist economy.

"Then again, we hear a lot about *democracy*, the dignity of man, and the socially responsible state. This reach for utopia is not wrong in itself but is really a very superficial effort at finding a solution. Actually, what is at issue here is a *question of power*. If we as workers and trade unions demand parity in the composition of the supervisory boards of big companies, it means we want to have a share of the power. We want to have a foot in the door.

"We are asking for more power, more influence for its own sake."

Asked about the tract at the 1974 Mitbestimmung hearings, Vetter of the labor federation said the piece was a polemic that was written in a purposely pointed style—"without grace or accoutrements." But he backed the underlying idea that partnership isn't possible without true equality of capital and labor.[15]

Chapter 4
Industrial Democracy in Other Countries

Throughout most of Western Europe, Mitbestimmung is looking very much like an idea whose time has come.

Since 1970, Denmark, Holland, Luxembourg, Austria, Sweden and Norway[1] have adopted worker-director programs for boards of major companies. The goverment-appointed Sudreau Commission in France has recommended what amounts to a French version of Mitbestimmung.

And in Britain, the government-appointed Industrial Democracy Committee headed by Lord Bullock was readying a report expected to recommend a form of board level co-determination for workers.

Parallel to these national efforts, the European Communities Commission, the administrative arm of the European Communities, has presented proposals for worker representation at board level in larger public companies in the Common Market.

The German example is spreading, though German Mitbestimmung models are being modified for adoption in other countries. There are holdouts too. In Switzerland, voters in a March 1976 national referendum specifically rejected the idea. Italy and Belgium have also stayed clear of co-determination.

The Common Market's proposals form a good starting point for a look at worker participation in Europe because they represent both a distillation of trends within some countries and because they will influence legislation yet to be introduced in other Common Market nations. The commission sees a good chance that its ideas will become law within the Common Market generally by 1980. If so, all present and future member nations would have to conform.

The commission so far as made two main proposals concerning worker co-determination. These are:

—Recommendations for a so-called Fifth Directive that would coordinate member-country laws dealing with joint stock, limited liability companies. The draft Fifth Directive, presented in 1972, would require all such companies to adopt a two-tier board system and would give seats on the supervisory board to workers or their representatives in all companies with at least 500 workers.

—A proposed "Statute for European Companies," made public in 1970 and amended in 1975. This proposal also foresees worker participation at supervisory-board level. The suggested statute has less immediate importance than the Fifth Directive, which is a proposal for far-reaching mandatory legislation, while the statute is suggested as an optional alternative corporate form for certain kinds of companies operating in more than one country.

The Fifth Directive, if it ever is to become binding on companies of European countries, must win the approval of the law-making body of the Common Market, the Council of Ministers, in which each member country effectively has a veto. It is far from certain if this approval will be obtained, but Common Market officials appear cautiously optimistic.

Edoardo Volpi, who was a division head in the Common Market Commission's Internal Market section, estimated in a 1976 interview that the Fifth Directive could become a reality by 1980. Volpi, who subsequently joined the External Relations section, ticked off the names of countries that had adopted worker-director systems since 1970. It is remarkable how fast opposition to worker co-determination can melt, he said.

"We started talking to the Dutch unions in 1965," he recalled. "They thought co-determination was a 'German disease' and they didn't like it." Five years later, they embraced it. The British Trades Union Congress opposed board-level representation in 1972, but now it wants the representation, he said.

The proposed Fifth Directive would give companies a choice of introducing board-level co-determination along the general lines of the German or Dutch models, the two systems in existence when the directive was being formulated. Under the German-type model, workers or their representatives would choose one-third of the supervisory board members. Under the Dutch-style system, the supervisory board itself would choose its own new members, but either the shareholders assembly or the workers could object to any particular appointment.

There is an error in page numbering and sequence in Chapter IV. Page 89 should be page 88; page 90 should be numbered page 89 and page 88 should be numbered page 90.

difficult to implement if those concerned, particularly those with a vested interest in existing systems and structures, are to participate in the decision making. However, for sophisticated, industrial societies, there is no alternative if they are to retain their democratic character. Difficult problems of industrial relations will be easier to solve properly, fairly and with a minimum of wasteful confrontation if there are mechanisms which involve those closely affected in the process of finding solutions. For, while such mechanisms cannot always produce complete agreement, they can at least help to ensure a reasonable degree of understanding and an adequate level of acceptance."

The commission considers the installation of worker-directors on corporate boards of directors to be the most important approach to worker participation. It recognizes three other approaches: Collective bargaining, establishing of worker representative bodies below the board level of companies, and share ownership by workers.

Collective bargaining traditionally has meant mainly bargaining about pay and fringe benefits, although work hours, holidays and settlement of disputes also figure in. But the European Commission conceded that the scope of collective bargaining has been increased in recent years in many countries to the point where it gives workers a voice reaching far beyond these traditional areas.

In Italy, for example, Fiat and Montedison concluded collective agreements that had clauses on such nontraditional matters as investment and employment levels. Management and unions in Great Britain often go beyond traditional collective-bargaining areas; many British collective agreements contain so-called status quo provisions that prevent the employer from making decisions affecting employees without first coming to an understanding with them or at least exhausting certain negotiating procedures.

The commission foresees further development of collective bargaining within the Common Market but doesn't think this method can provide a substitute for board-level co-determination. Several reasons are offered for the indispensibility of worker-directors.

First, the results of collective bargaining inevitably depend on the relative strengths of the bargaining parties, which makes

The Dutch-style system would allow objections to be made on one of two grounds—that a candidate was unqualified or that his appointment would harm the balanced composition of the board. In the event of an objection, the appointment couldn't take effect unless the complaint were ruled unjustified by an independent outside body.

The proposed Fifth Directive obviously has been around for a while without finding acceptance. The Common Market's economic and social committee—representing employers, employees and the public interest—was completely divided on the proposal. Another obstacle to acceptance was the enlargement of the Common Market in 1973 by the additional memberships of Britain, Ireland and Denmark. The enlargement brought into the Common Market new viewpoints and traditions that would have to be integrated into any scheme for harmonizing company law.

Ultimately, the Common Market Commission must go back to the drawing boards. It has tried to stimulate discussion of problems of co-determination to seek a consensus as the basis for a revised proposal.

The opening statement in this discussion came from the European Commission in the form of a "Green Paper" published in 1975. The document, called *Employee Participation and Company Structure,*[2] doesn't make specific proposals but reaffirms the commission's commitment to the installation of voting worker-directors on the supervisory boards of major companies operating in Common Market countries. It concedes the need for flexibility about the timing of this arrangement and the necessity for allowing companies latitude in their approach toward these goals.

The commission argues in the Green Paper that joint European Communities company law is needed to create a "common market for companies"—a legal environment that facilitates cross-national business activities like mergers and investments. In creating this common market for companies, the commission wrote in a sort of co-determination manifesto, due regard must be paid to two "important evolutions."

The first: "The increasing recognition being given to the democratic imperative that those who will be substantially affected by decisions made by social and political institutions must be involved in the making of those decisions. In particular, employees are increasingly seen to have interests in the functioning of enterprises which can be as substantial as those of shareholders, and sometimes more so. Employees not only derive their income from enterprises which employ them but they devote a large proportion of their daily lives to the enterprise.

"Decisions taken by or in the enterprise can have a substantial effect on their economic circumstances, both immediately and in the longer term; the satisfaction which they derive from their work; their health and physical condition; the time and energy which they can devote to their families and to activities other than work; and even their sense of dignity and autonomy as human beings. Accordingly, continuing consideration is being given to the problem of how and to what extent employees should be able to influence the decisions of enterprises which employ them."

The second "evolution" cited by the commission: "A growing awareness of the need for institutions which can respond effectively to the need for change. This awareness is based upon the perception that the present era is one characterized by change, and that this feature may well become more pronounced in years to come. Changes in the economic environment, sometimes of a radical nature, like the recent sharp rise in energy prices, are bound to confront the Community in the future, probably with increasing frequency. As far as industrial affairs are concerned, the difficult situations which have arisen in several Member States as a result of the impact of basic technological changes on long established industries and their associated communities have dramatically emphasized the trend. And it is clear that the completion and operation of the European Community will itself involve structural changes of a substantial kind. All member states without exception are thus faced with the prospect of having to implement changes, sometimes of a radical nature, as regards their economic and social structures, both immediately and for the foreseeable future."

Is there any contradiction between "the democratic imperative" and the need to gear up for change? The European Commission said, "In some ways, there is a degree of tension between these two developments. Changes which are desirable from a broad economic and social point of view may appear to be more for an "inherent variability" that isn't considered compatible with bringing about minimum standards of worker participation in the Community. Some unions simply don't have the power they need to create any significant changes, the commission said. Even strong unions may not be able to convince their members that participation is an issue worth fighting for.

Second, it is difficult to formulate any general law requiring companies to bargain about participation matters. Any attempt to legislate in this area would be hard to interpret in practice, the commission said.

Third, the commission said, "expansion of the scope of collective bargaining necessarily increases the number of issues that may lead to confrontation. But industrial confrontation is wasteful, and if it occurs too often in a society, every member of that society is the poorer, including those who are employees."

Similarly, the commission called employee representation below board level a useful tool for many purposes—for example, making sure that the "human aspects" of the production process always are drawn into management considerations. But it argued that because such representation—whether in works councils, shop stewards' committees or mixed worker-management committees—is "external to the decision-making bodies of the company, their effectiveness may well be questioned." It added, "On the other hand, to give strong legal powers to such institutions in relation to the enterprise's economic decision-making, for example the right to veto, is to risk paralyzing the enterprise as a business organization."

As to worker ownership of the shares of the companies for which they work, the commission said that such schemes as exist within the Common Market don't give workers any real influence in decision-making. It said that the "time has not yet come" for Common Market legislation in this area.

Thus, nothing can substitute for worker-directors, in the commission's view. It noted that fears of such a system exist both among labor and business leaders. Labor in some countries fears that board-level participation will replace struggle with class collaboration, or that the position of the unions will be undermined by creation of an apparatus that is independent of them. Some business leaders oppose worker-directors on the ground that these directors will use their positions to further the class struggle or to seriously weaken the company's hand in dealing with the unions.

Against these arguments, the commission contended that board-level participation is the only one of the four existing participation methods that involves the worker on a continuous basis in strategic decision-making at the highest level of the company. This involvement, by increasing workers' information and improving the experience and understanding of those involved, is "likely to have a positive, if indirect, effect on the process of collective bargaining," the commission said.

The European Commission rejects arguments that employee participation will cut industrial efficiency by leading firms to preserve existing business structures and jobs rather than innovating. It said, "If one compares the positions in the different member states, it certainly cannot be said that there is an apparent correlation between regimes of employee participation and situations of low efficiency, low profits and inadequate investment.

"If anything, these problems seem more closely associated with the existence of industrial relations systems in which there is little or no formal employee participation and a relatively high incidence of industrial confrontation. Though a causal connection cannot be scientifically established, this observation would suggest that social conflict, resulting in part from the exclusion of employees from decision-making, is a greater threat to efficiency and investment than a degree of employee participation."

Edoardo Volpi of the European Commission concluded: Countries may try worker participation and find "it is not a good thing. But until now, it has gone hand-in-hand with better industrial relations. This is a trend."

Worker participation in management is a fast-developing story in Europe. Although the German system is the point of departure for most of the other programs, some aspects of the systems in the European Community and a few other countries help put the German system into perspective and illustrate the national variations. Because the developments have been changing so rapidly, the view here will be arbitrarily limited to three countries—Sweden, Britain and France as of late 1976.

Discussion of industrial democracy has been reverberating

in Sweden since 1968, when a series of books critized working conditions in Swedish firms. The books renewed a debate, dating to the beginning of the century, about how to give workers a bigger voice in company decision-making. A major strike at the state-owned LKAB mines in 1969 heated up the discussion and led to a new legislation, including:

—An "Act on Co-Determination at Work," effective Jan. 1, 1977, that opens almost all aspects of management to collective bargaining on increasing workers' influence.

—Laws passed in 1976 giving workers two voting seats on most boards of directors in companies with at least 25 workers. (Swedish boards are similar to American ones, rather than two-tier).

In the background, a debate rages about plans for increasing union ownership of industry.

The Co-Determination Act, applying to almost all employers, has as its centerpiece a "Paragraph 32" provision that dramatically widens collective bargaining in the area of co-determination. It is this paragraph that give unions the right to bargain for co-determination in almost any aspect of management.

The number assigned to this paragraph has significance in Swedish industrial relations. Until the new law was framed, the "32" was associated with the 32nd article of the Constitution of the Swedish Employers Confederation (SAF), which sharply limited the permitted content of collective bargaining agreements reached by the confederation's member companies.

The confederation's Article 32 obliged the organization's members to submit drafts of all agreements reached with the unions to the confederation's board for approval. No agreement could be signed without the board's consent, and violations of this rule could entail fines for the offending employer.

A juxtaposition of the new Paragraph 32 with the relevant sections of the SAF's Article 32, now of very limited significance, underlines the turnabout.

New Paragraph 32 of the Co-Determination law:

"Between parties to a collective agreement on pay and general conditions of employment there should, if the union side so requests, also be concluded a collective agreement on co-determination for employees in questions relating to concluding and canceling employment contracts, to supervision and distribution of work or to other aspects of management."[3]

Excerpt of Article 32 of the employers' Constitution:

"Collective contracts concluded between a part-owner or member of the confederation and a trade union federation must contain the provision stipulating the right of the employer to engage and dismiss workers at his own discretion; to direct and allot the work; and to avail himself of workers belonging to any organization whatever, or to none."[4] The rule had been stretched in the past, but nevertheless remained an important guideline.

In essence, the new "32" places management's old prerogatives in the center of the bargaining table. Paragraph 44 of the new law extends the rights granted by Paragraph 32. It allows workers to strike for co-determination rights even when a collective agreement on wages is in effect, provided co-determination questions remain outstanding at the close of wage negotiations.

What actually comes out of co-determination negotiations will depend on the relative bargaining power of management and unions and the degree to which unions can interest their members in making co-determination demands.

The new law applies almost universally, with the exception of activities that are of a "religious, scientific, artistic or of some other idealistic nature or the purpose of which is cooperative, trade union, political or otherwise opinion-forming." In the case of government activities, the principle of co-determination must respect the right of political control. For example, government workers won't be allowed to make tax policy or determine educational aims.

Despite the law's theoretically almost unlimited potential for placing management prerogatives in the hands of workers, talks with union, employer and government officials indicate there won't be any immediate revolutionary effects. Mrs. Birgitta Isaksson, secretary of the Committee on Democratization of the white-collar workers union, said, "Change will be slow in the beginning. There must be time to experiment in this new field."

Another observer says, "You must not expect drastic results at first. There will be co-determination agreements relating to the shop floor, but not much at the top level." Tore Lidbom, an ombudsman at the blue-collar workers union, said the items of most importance to unions at the beginning will be in the area of personnel policy, work organization, information, and computers.

Initially, the union may seek rights for unions to appoint personnel managers in companies, to establish "autonomous" worker groups in companies that would have power over working conditions, and to limit certain management uses of computers. Unions may seek, for example, to curb the compiling of computerized files with personal information about workers' habits and problems.

Lennart Grafström, assistant to the director of the employers' confederation, said he believed the unions would have some difficulties persuading their members to strike or threaten to strike over co-determination issues. There's a lag between the conception of ideas in central-union headquarters and the acceptance of those ideas at local level, he said. In addition, he suggested that the upset defeat of the Social Democratic Party in the 1976 election might hurt unions' bargaining power. Some Swedish observers indicated that unions used their influence with the government in the past to achieve through legislation or the treat of legislation concessions they couldn't win through collective bargaining.

The Swedish word for "co-determination," (Medbestämmande), in the new act has a less definite meaning than Mitbestimmung has in German usage. Olof Bergqvist, a division chief in the Ministry of Labor, said Medbestämmande negotiations could go beyond the meaning of "Mitbestimmung"—i.e., an equal voice of labor and management. Labor could win the final say in some areas, he contends. Union ombudsman Lidbom adds that workers will seek some powers of final decision and some veto rights, while contenting themselves with consultative participation in other areas.

Paragraph 32 is the most spectacular part of the new act. Other significant points include:

—Employers are obliged to initiate negotiations with unions on major operational changes or on conditions of work or employment. Implementation of such changes must await the completion of negotiations unless there are "extraordinary reasons" for going ahead immediately. Grafström said the law doesn't mean that managements have to come to an agreed solution with the unions, except where a collective co-determination pact so specifies. In most cases, the final decision lies with the employer. But he noted that the power of unions to delay in itself gives them some bargaining power. A delayed decision may be as good as none for the union.

—On all other questions, unions may demand negotiations on a local and national basis. In such cases, the employer again must postpone execution of his decision unless there are special reasons for speed.

—The employer, on his own initiative, must inform trade unions continuously on economic and operational developments and personnel policy. The trade union has the right to inspect books, accounts and other documents and to request studies on matters about which they need information. Disputes about whether the information received is to be treated as confidential are to be resolved by bargaining. Lack of agreement entitles the employer to apply to the labor court for a ruling. But even "confidential" information may be passed to the executive of the national trade union.

—In disputes concerning agreements on co-determination, the interpretation of the union shall be accepted until the dispute is finally settled.

Board-level worker participation tends to arouse little controversy in Sweden. It generally is considered, in the words of Grafström of the employers' confederation—"one small part of industrial democracy."[5] The unions appear satisfied with the minority representation assigned to them under the law and look to the new Paragraph 32 of the co-determination act to provide significant gains in participation.

The legislation on worker-directors was adopted after a three-year period of experimentation under temporary laws introduced in 1973. The new legislation generally gives unions representing workers in a firm or cooperative association with at least 25 employees the right to name two voting directors and two nonvoting deputy directors.

The German unions' drive toward parity representation on company boards isn't duplicated in Sweden at this time. Said Mrs. Isaksson of the white-collar union: "Board-level participation was the first thing but it's not the biggest thing. It's a complement." She said her union believes shareholders must retain control of the board. Worker control of boards without ownership would imply in her words "power without means." Besides, unions are freer to criticize when they don't have control or an equal voice, she added.

Lidbom of the blue-collar union thinks the worker-director plan has definite uses for unions, but he too is satisfied with a minority role on the board. He said that board participation enables workers to get information not otherwise available and to discuss their problems directly with shareholder representatives rather than having to rely on the managing director to relay their thoughts. But he said the area of key interest to unions is "work organization"—conditions of work immediately affecting members—and this area is largely outside the board's purview.

The Swedish system emerging from the new laws on board-level representation and co-determination obviously will have some similarities to the German system of worker participation in the Aufsichtsrat and Betriebsrat, but the emphasis in the Swedish system is much less legalistic than in the German program. Bergqvist said the team that drafted the Swedish legislation studied the German system closely but quickly became convinced that "this was not the medicine we wanted."

The Swedish system is designed to emphasize negotiations by the unions. If the German system were applied in Sweden, it could result in an institution that competes with collective bargaining and weakens the role of the unions, he said.

Burgeoning Swedish industrial democracy is accompanied by a vigorous debate over "economic democracy"—or how to give workers a bigger share of ownership of the economy. The blue-collar union's congress in June 1976 endorsed a proposal by Dr. Rudolf Meidner, a leading economist, for a thoroughgoing redistribution of company wealth in favor of the workers. The plan probably is the most radical of its type to win serious consideration in a Western country.

The Meidner program essentially would require companies to allocate 20% of their pretax profit annually to collective employee funds, controlled by trade unions.[6] The union's endorsement of the proposal was an apparent embarrassment to the Social Democratic Party, which said that the Meidner plan would need several years' investigation. The Social Democrats' defeat in the fall 1976 elections probably represented a major setback for the plan.

In Britain, the nine-member Bullock Committee on Industrial Democracy has been preparing recommendations intended to serve as the basis for a "radical extension of industrial democracy."

The committee, appointed in December 1975, is headed by Lord Bullock, an Oxford University historian whose works include *Hitler, A Study of Tyranny* and *The Life and Times of Ernest Bevin.* It includes representatives from banking, industry, academic life, the trade union movement and the legal profession.

The committee was expected to come up with proposals for some form of mandatory worker participation on company boards, but it wasn't certain how close it would come up to demands for parity representation made by the 11 million-member Trades Union Congress. What appeared certain was that any form of mandatory participation would meet with the displeasure of the employers association, the Confederation of British Industry. The confederation had accepted the need for an extension of industrial democracy but felt this end could be furthered best by negotiated co-determination agreements that only rarely would provide for worker representation on boards.

The spreading of industrial democracy in Britain poses special problems. The country has long suffered from forms of class war between employer and employee that was immortalized in the film, *I'm All Right Jack.* Secondly, the labor movement is characterized by a multiplicity of unions operating within each industrial sector. E. J. Robertson, director of social affairs for the industry confederation, said that as many as 20 separate unions sometimes operate within a single British company.

The questions then are: Will industrial democracy merely spread class war? Can the myriad separate unions operating within a company show enough interunion cooperation to share responsibility with management and shareholders for running a company?

The unions obviously think neither of these problems is insurmountable. Industry is dubious.

David Lea, head of the Trades Union Congress economics department and a member of the Bullock Committee, said that until a few years ago, British unions had essentially the same attitude toward board-level participation as their American counterparts—they didn't want to compromise their freedom by becoming involved in company policy-making. This has given way to a desire to become involved, he contended.

As the Trades Union Congress put it in evidence to the committee, "It is increasingly evident that the major issues determined by boards of directors are of close interest to work-people. . . . These include the appointment of top management, disposition of resources, mergers and the acquisition and disposal of assets. Work-people should have a right to a say in such decisions, at present reserved to the shareholders."[7]

The change in the Trades Union Congress attitude, not shared by all British unions, resulted in the Labor government's decision to set up the Bullock Committee. Labor Secretary Peter Shore gave the committee a tightly worded assignment. The assignment, known as the committee's "Terms of References":

"Accepting the need for a radical extension of industrial democracy in the control of companies [in the private sector] by means of representation on boards of directors, and accepting the essential role of trade union organizations in this process, to consider how such an extension can best be achieved, taking into account in particular the proposals of the Trades Union Congress . . . as well as experience in Britain . . . and other countries. Having regard to the interest of the national economy, employees, investors and consumers to analyze the implications of such representation for the efficient management of companies and for company law."[8]

The assignment assumed the need for more industrial democracy, the necessity to accomplish this through board-level representation and the central role of the unions in the matter. "Industry feels the terms of reference for the inquiry were unhelpful," said C. Hawksworth, manager of the industry confederation's social affairs research department. "Some say scurrilous."

Whatever the committee came up with, it could hardly be a compromise pleasing to both sides. The alternative proposals put forward by the Trades Union Congress and industry confederation have almost no overlap.

The unions wanted nothing less than complete parity representation. It told the committee: "It is the TUC view that it is unrealistic to expect 'equal responsibility' without 'equal representation.' Nothing could be more damaging than having to accept responsibility if the shareholders' representatives had an entrenched majority. Only with a system of parity representation can trade union representatives be expected to feel any sense of collective responsibility for board decisions."[9]

The Trades Union Congress would resolve any board deadlocks by giving a tie-breaking vote to a chairman alternating between worker and shareholder representatives, or by calling in an outsider, or by joint "cooptation" of the chairman, or through an independent chairman. It began by advocating that Britain's current unity board system be replaced by two-tier boards, but later it stopped insisting on this.

The plan of the Trades Union Congress would apply initially to the more than 700 companies that have at least 2,000 workers, with further progressions down to the 200-worker level made by parliamentary vote. Unions would choose worker representatives and allot seats among themselves. Because not all unions want representation, the system would come into being only if unions demanded it.

The German influence on the British proposals is quite clear. The demand for equal representation on a two-tier board and the 2,000-worker limit for companies initially affected by this representation are almost exact duplicates. The TUC's David Lea conceded this, saying, "The German example is well known to us all." But he added, "We were aware of its strengths and weaknesses. We didn't want to buy the whole package."

For one thing, the British model is wholly based on trade unions naming board members, whereas German workers themselves under the new law choose directly or through elected representatives the majority of their representatives. For another, the TUC would find unacceptable separate representation for the "leitende Angestellte." (Here Lea, like many other Britons discussing co-determination, used the German words.)

He said he personally asked many German companies what proportion of their payrolls represented the leitenden Angestellten. "They said 2%, 3%, or 4%," he said. To give the leitenden Angestellten separate seats, he contended, is "arithmetically outrageous."

Lea says the Trades Union Congress isn't looking beyond parity representation. "Our current policy is equality," he said. "This seems like a natural concept. Both labor and capital are necessary to production."

He added that the various unions operating within single companies would have "no problem" agreeing on splitting up the worker seats among themselves. He disagreed with the view that Mitbestimmung is a good way to preserve consensus about the economy but not a good way to create it.

He said, "If you want consensus, you've got to get workers involved. You've got to construct a framework for joint action." He said unions will act "more responsibly" when integrated into a company's decision-making process.

The Confederation of British Industry had other ideas. In its evidence to the Bullock Committee, it said flatly: "Any suggestion that employee participation necessarily involves employee 'delegates' on the board is irrelevant and unacceptable." It argued that the objectives set out in the Trades Union Congress document "Industrial Democracy," including parity board level representation, "are in direct opposition to the national interest. These proposals would be detrimental to Britain's already weak economy because . . . they would interfere with the achievement of the basic task of all employers and managers, namely the optimum use of resources in the interest of employees, investors and consumers."[10]

The employers organization nevertheless agreed that "greater employee participation" could be of help to the economy. And it made a plea for a "flexible approach" to participation, based on negotiated agreements in each company with more than 2,000 workers.

Under the confederation plan, such companies would be given four years to reach "participation agreements" with their employees. If no agreement were reached within this period, the case would be referred to "specially designed tribunals" empowered to submit it to compulsory arbitration. The overall aim of the agreements would be to promote the employee's "involvement" in his job by giving him more information about the job in relation to the company's objectives, the business situation of the company and the reasons for major company decisions affecting employees.

Once having been ratified by the majority of employees under a secret ballot, the agreements would remain in effect for three years. The accords would have to ensure commercial secrecy and couldn't "interfere with the executive function of management." The agreements in theory could result in some employee participation at board level either on a supervisory board or on a unitary board, but this "usually will not be a suitable form of participation."

The confederation said the agreements might lead to creation of such institutions as company councils, plant or subsidiary councils, non-executive directors to whom employee representatives have special access and trustee advisory boards.

The virtue of its proposals, the confederation contended, is that they would lead to individual, agreed solutions best tailored to each company and would avoid the imposition of one rigid legal form of participation on the many forms of companies in Britain.

Why can't the German idea of board-level participation work in England? E. J. Robertson of the industry confederation replied, "The German unions are rich, business-minded and supportive of the capitalistic system." He left the rest unsaid but nodded in agreement when it was suggested that there is less consensus in Britain than in Germany about the aims of the economy.

Confederation officials appeared resigned to the probability that the Bullock Committee would recommend some form of compulsory worker-directors but were hoping it would be something other than the "worst possible outcome"—parity representation with unions in total control of the worker side. "A lot of our members are keen to fight the committee's proposals, but we'll have to wait to see what these proposals are first," said C. Hawksworth.

The officials also hoped that, despite the narrowness of the committee's terms of reference, the committee would adopt their proposals for below-board-level participation.

No matter what the committee decided, the future of worker participation in Britain would remain uncertain. The "whole program is dependent on the Labor government remaining in office," said an official close to the committee. "A Conservative government would throw everything back into the melting pot."

In France, the seeds of co-determination have been planted, but the harvest is uncertain.

Since 1945, public limited-liability companies (sociétés anonymes) with at least 50 employees have been required to give two nonvoting seats on their board to employees. Beginning in 1972, this number was increased to four in companies having a supervisory and technical staff of more than 24. In government-owned industry, one-third of the voting seats belong to employees.

In February 1975, a government-appointed commission headed by Parliamentary Deputy Pierre Sudreau proposed an extension of board-level worker participation, a recommendation that produced considerable discussion and hints of coming legislation.

President Valery Giscard d'Estaing and Labor Minister Michel Durafour announced in April 1976 they planned to introduce legislation establishing a framework for greater worker participation on boards. However, work on actual proposals went onto the back burner in the face of opposition from employers and unions.

Late in 1976, the whole matter remained a subject of public debate, centered on the Sudreau Report. This 60,000-word study enjoyed a remarkably brisk sale of some 150,000 copies.[11] The heavy turnover illustrated the "need for this type of thinking," a source close to the commission said.

"Some people say the proposals are too timid," he said. "Others say they're a revolution. It is too early to say what will come of them."

Judged against the background of European debate, the Sudreau proposals look anything but revolutionary. Nevertheless, they were startling to a country noted for its authoritarian management system. The small and medium-size French firms are run "on the principle of the divine right of the employer to decide the fate of the company and all those who work for it," an American observer said. The major companies are somewhat more liberal but far less so than their German counterparts.

The Sudreau report was framed by realists, who took this state of affairs into account. A basic principle pervading the report's recommendations on participation is that company decisions ultimately must be taken by "one man," even though the commission held that preparation of the decision should be multi-sided. For this reason, the commission suggested that only minority board-level participation be introduced for workers—one-third is the figure it speaks of—and that the introduction be gradual and flexible.

The commission specifically rejected German co-determination in the sense of an equal labor voice with capital. To avoid any contamination by German model, it used the word "co-supervision" rather than "co-determination" to describe its concept.

The commission agreed that participation would be entirely optional for smaller companies—to be defined either as those with less than 2,000 or less than 1,000 workers. It said: "Some members [of the commission] were of the opinion that co-supervision should remain entirely optional [for big companies] in the immediate term and in the future. Others, on the other hand, opted for making co-supervision compulsory in large companies after a five year period. . . ."[12]

Participation could be either within the two-tier board system—at present little used in France—or on a unitary board that was modified to distinguish clearly between the board's twin responsibilities of supervision and day-to-day management.

The report suggests that all classes of employees—manual, clerical, supervisory-technical, and middle and senior management—should be allowed to have a hand in selection of board members. Supervisory and middle-management grades would always have two representatives.

Several possible methods of selection of these representatives are suggested:

—Giving voting rights to the workers who already sit on boards in a purely consultative capacity. Such workers are chosen by the works council.

—Appointment by the unions.

—Election by the entire work force of candidates chosen by the unions. If the number of votes cast on the first ballot were less than half of the number of registered voters, nominations would be thrown open.

—Election by the entire work force with the nominations open from the outset.

The commission said the questions need debate.

The board-level participation recommendations form half of the commission's recommendations for creating a bigger role for workers in French company life. The commission also suggests widening the scope of collective bargaining to give workers more say over working conditions and more room for "innovation," for example, in the creation of new types of institutions to represent workers.

It also suggests strengthening of works councils. Such councils, which are legally required to be set up in all companies employing more than 50 workers, consist of delegates elected by employees and of the company chief executive. The councils, required under a 1945 law introduced by Gen. Charles de Gaulle, were intended by de Gaulle to play a major part in representing workers' interest in the company. But employers have helped push the councils into a rather narrow role—concentrating on the administration of company welfare and leisure activities.

The Sudreau report noted that half the companies required to establish such councils haven't done so. It suggests a "thorough application of the law" both as regards establishment of the councils and widening of their use of their theoretical powers. One suggestion is to promote the flow of economic information to the workers by forming small "economic committees" within the councils that would meet frequently with management to discuss the company's economic condition.

The commission specifically rejected the possibility of giving works councils a veto over certain types of company decisions, such as hiring and firing and general personnel policy, as in the German Betriebsrat system. It said: "In the absence of a minimum consensus between the partners, such a procedure, which imposes considerable constraints, would be incompatible with the need for decisions to be taken with speed and by a single authority."[13]

John Condon, labor attaché at the U.S. Embassy in Paris, said it was likely that the Sudreau recommendations on board-level participation would be bypassed because of their general unpopularity. The biggest trade union, the communist Confédération Générale du Travail (CGT), is staunchly opposed to the proposals.

Condon explained, "The unions are very ideological in their approach to life. They are very much attached to the adversary principle. So is the AFL-CIO. Only here it's put a little differently. The unions here are against 'class collaboration.' "

Also weighing in against the proposals was the employers association, Le Conseil National du Patronat Francaise.

Condon said, "The government would be well advised not to push this because there are other, more meaningful possible reforms." He said he personally considers the German Mitbestimmung model "passé." What really matters to workers, he said, is the "nature of the relationships at the work place." Improvements in this area call for an intensification of worker participation below the board level, he suggested.

Others are not so sure. A well-placed French source, who asked not to be identified noted that French unions have tended in the past to distain particular reforms in favor of a reform of society as a whole. Management and employers have tended to try to "preserve what they've got rather than look ahead." But these attitudes aren't necessarily immutable, he contended.

"If we exclude the political problems of the moment," he said, "there is a large interest in participation. If the unions get the [board-level] power, they will be forced to play the game. And the employers aren't really solidly against the proposals. The top people at the [employer's association] and in the big companies say the proposals are okay. Their public statements reflect the need to speak for small and medium size firms as well."

This source said that the Sudreau report is an attempt, unique in recent French history, to accomplish company reform in the absence of crises such as those in 1936, 1945 and 1968 that accompanied previous reforms. He said: "Employers and employees are asked to conceive of the company as something different from a simple property or as a cockpit for struggle among the classes. They are asked to see the company as a place to live and work together with solidarity on some points and differences on others. The theme of the report is that the company is the basic cell of society. This is something new to the French mentality."

He admitted there are risks in the committee's recommendations. "Co-supervision will have effects on the level and rhythm of economic growth," he conceded. "Capital is versatile and risk-taking. If you have a bigger labor voice, you can go progressively to decisions that emphasize security. . . . Perhaps the worst possible fate would be to go along without participation because a society like France could explode. Maybe noncompetitive companies are the worst possible fate. But the commission feels it [co-supervision] is worth the risk because it can strengthen companies, putting the emphasis on the solidarity of shareholders and workers."

He said participation also can be an antidote to calls for nationalization of various industries, like steel and autos. "If a company is just an owned thing, then it's easy to go to nationalization. You just change ownership. If it's more than an owned thing, it is harder to nationalize."

Experience in Switzerland suggests that co-determination isn't necessarily an irresistible force. On March 21, 1976, Switzerland held a referendum on a proposal by the Swiss Trade Union Federation to amend the nation's constitution to allow the government to "legislate on the co-determination of employees and their organizations in enterprises, management and administration."

The federation said its aim was to humanize work, increase worker motivation and pave the way for ultimate worker participation on a parity basis. Industry representatives argued that passage would give the unions a lever to dethrone the private economy and replace it by a socialist industrial system.

The proposal was defeated by a two-to-one margin.

But the Swiss can hardly be described as trendy. It wasn't until 1971 that Swiss women got the vote. As Ezio Canonica, president of the Trade Union Federation, said in a sober, prereferendum commentary, "the Swiss are like alpinists who want to be sure that every step up is sure."[14]

Chapter 5
Mitbestimmung and the U.S.

The European Mitbestimmung boom has left the U.S. largely untouched, but it is hard to quarrel with the assessment of U.S. publications like Barron's[1] and Fortune[2] that the idea is bound to get more American attention in the future.

The first real American nibble at something like formal co-determination came when the United Auto Workers sought two seats on the board of Chrysler Corp. as part of its 1976 negotiating package. The demand was dropped when management resisted, but in the words of a union official, "We planted the seed." The idea is likely to come up again in the future, at Chrysler or elsewhere in the U.S.

The main reason why board-level worker representation hasn't been debated thoroughly in the U.S. up to now is that most American unions oppose it (the UAW is an exception). They see the idea as:

—A potential threat to union strength because the board representatives might be independent of organized labor.

—Inimical to the "adversary relationship" between U.S. unions and management.

—Superfluous in light of the "worker participation" achieved by U.S. labor through collective bargaining.

They are much the same reasons for which British unions opposed Mitbestimmung until recently.

The traditional U.S. labor case against Mitbestimmung is well put by Irving Brown, the AFL-CIO's Paris-based European representative and a member of the governing body of the International Labor Organization in Geneva.

Brown affirmed that most U.S. unions are antipathetic or indifferent to labor participation on company boards of directors. "But most of our people feel that they are achieving what is known as 'worker participation' through collective bargaining. In other words, there are decisions made in plants now jointly by employers and unions on matters that 30 or 50 years ago would have been called management prerogatives."

He noted that employers in the construction, shipping and printing industries are free to hire whom they want only after they have checked to find whether the union can supply an applicant. In the coal mining and clothing industries, unions have a major say in setting piece rates. Organized labor in the coal mining, chemical and rubber industries is active in safety and health matters, he contended. These areas were once wholly in the domain of employers.

If unions are strong, labor's influence can extend beyond factory walls to include the relationship of the factory to the community, he said. Air and water pollution by an employer might be challenged by a strong union.

"In other words," he added, "over the years, the whole range of participation by the unions has grown beyond what we used to call 'bread-and-butter' issues."

Brown's words called to mind the European Communities Commission's observation that results of collective bargaining show "inherent variability" because they ultimately depend on the relative strengths of individual pairs of bargaining parties. The commission rejected collective bargaining as a substitute for board-level co-determination. Did Brown feel U.S. unions were right to rely on their own strength for results?

He contended it is better for unions to trust their own strength than to depend for progress on passage of pro-labor laws by the political party in power. He noted that the German unions were forced to accept a Mitbestimmung bill that they considered unsatisfactory because Chancellor Helmut Schmidt's Social Democratic Party had to compromise with its Free Democratic coalition partners.

What's more, he added, a "different government of a different nature possibly could change the law." U.S. unions don't depend on any one political party, he said; their fortunes don't depend basically on which party is in office.

Brown suggested that the remedy for union weaknesses, for example in the Southern U.S. and among white-collar workers, is worker and union action to strengthen them, rather than new laws. Legislation has a role to play in establishing "vital minimums, but if workers want to go beyond this, they have to do something about it," he said.

Wouldn't board membership offer unions valuable information? Brown answered, "Our people want more information, and they're getting more." But the AFL-CIO opposes board-level representation because it might tend to "diffuse" union power and because it would blur traditional distinctions between workers and management.

With regard to the first point, he noted that worker representation in the U.S. is handled exclusively by the unions. There is a marked reluctance to risk any sharing of union duties, responsibilities and power, he said.

Moreover, he said, "If you begin to move into management in the formal sense, then you have the responsibility for management, and sometimes you find yourself on both sides of the table. We say the workers are the workers and the employers are the employers, and they both have different interests in terms of representation, and the democratic way is to reach a compromise and gradually work toward common goals—but not by giving up our rights. We also don't have management giving up their rights either."

Brown noted that the UAW bid for seats on the Chrysler board differed fundamentally from the German system in that the UAW sought its seats through collective bargaining rather than through legislation. But he still doesn't see other unions copying the UAW unless the economy takes a disastrous downward turn. Such an event might provoke calls for board representation or nationalization, he said.

Brown's skepticism is shared by other top AFL-CIO leaders. Thomas R. Donahue, executive assistant to AFL-CIO President George Meany, said that if unions were to become a "partner in management" they would be "most likely the junior partner in success and the senior partner in failure."[3] He said unions influence more issues through collective bargaining than they could hope to affect as board members.

VW personnel manager Peter Frerk said of this attitude, "The only thing Meany knows is management versus labor. Maybe things will change when Meany leaves office." But things look different from the point of view of the UAW, which seceded from the AFL-CIO in 1968 as a result of policy and personality differences.

Discussing the United Auto Workers request for board-level participation, Jerry Dale, assistant UAW public relations director, said the union felt that if workers had sat on the Chrysler board in 1974, they might have helped the company avoid the massive post-Thanksgiving 1974 layoff, when more than half the Chrysler work force was sent home. The move led to exhaustion of the company's supplemental unemployment benefits fund for workers.

Dale said Chrysler ignored economic warning signals in 1974 and kept increasing inventories until drastic measures had to be taken. He said the UAW reasoned that "if we'd had a couple of people on the board, we might have prevented the tragedy that occurred" by calling more attention to signs of impending trouble. At present, the union does not have any regular access to the board. It normally deals with management through industrial relations executives. Although there are rare meetings between top-level union and company officials, "we never deal with the board of directors," he said.

The board-level participation demand was seen as a way to allow the union to express opinions directly to the board, Dale said. It wasn't thought of as a first step toward equal labor-management responsibility on the board, which the union doesn't want, he said.

The UAW didn't push the issue hard when management resisted. It wasn't a "major demand" or a "strikeable issue," Dale said. But he said, "We have planted the seed," and he added it's quite possible the demand will come up again.

Leonard Woodcock, President of the UAW, said in the spring of 1976 that he was impressed by the conditions that VW workers were able to impose on the automaker's plan to assemble cars in the U.S. The case showed that the Mitbestimmung system "obviously has value," he said.

"Historically," he said, "unions have had to fight for their existence in the U.S. It's been US and THEM." But things are changing. He said "Ten or fifteen years ago, co-determination would have been viewed as a sellout by the unions. This isn't true anymore." He said that 1973 UAW contracts had provided for the establishment of joint worker-management committees that over a period of time would prove the two sides can have common interests, that "you don't have to have an adversary relationship."

Herman Rebhan, formerly chief of the UAW's foreign affairs department and now general secretary of the International Metalworkers Federation in Geneva, said he foresees American workers moving toward board participation in the next 10 years. Major factors impelling them in this direction, he said, are a desire for early information and influence on major company decisions like plant relocations and the need for union-management cooperation in job enrichment.

Rebhan said American unions "aren't ideologically oriented" like their European counterparts and won't try to justify board participation as part of a plan to reform capitalism. The movement toward participation will arise from pragmatic considerations, he said. "It will come, for example, when workers say 'Look, we've got to have something to say about the way a plant closes down, how a plant moves, and who moves or what,' " he said.

The contraction of the German coal industry was more favorable to workers because employers couldn't carry it out "unilaterally," he said.

Board participation would give American workers "early information and some input on these questions," he said. Does he fear that such a role for workers would compromise labor's independence? "Why should it?" he said. "After all, we sit together on pension boards. We sit together on other boards."

Well, for example, you might be inhibited in your wage claims if you knew exactly what a company was making, it was suggested.

"On the other hand, you may make an intelligent wage demand," he countered. "It works both ways. Anyone can make a wage demand, you know. But can you make an intelligent one?"

He noted, however, there is a recurrent suspicion among U.S. unions that management might try to use an introduction of board-level participation as a means of reducing union power. "Unions in Sweden and Germany don't have to worry about this because management there has accepted the unions," he said. "In the U.S. to this date, management tolerates us, has to deal with us, but I don't think they have philosophically accepted the unions."

Rebhan said a recent drive toward job enrichment—reducing the monotony of assembly-line work—can be expected to help foster the idea of union-management cooperation and soften the adversary relationship, smoothing the way for board-level participation. He said 1973 UAW contracts established joint committees on job enrichment that have been conducting thousands of quiet experiments at Ford, General Motors and Chrysler.

Job enrichment can't be handled by collective bargaining alone, he said. "You can't sit there and negotiate to a 12 o'clock deadline. It's an evolutionary process. You have to have trust in each other." While these job-enrichment committees don't involve board-level participation, they should help alter union-management attitudes toward each other, he said.

Rebhan said it is "too early" to discuss any legislation to establish worker-directors. Woodcock said, though, that legislative backup would be necessary if board-level Mitbestimmung were to gain "any standing" because employers could be expected to oppose the trend.

While both Woodcock and Rebhan basically were favorable to board-level participation, neither was enthusiastic about the German works-council system. "It must be seen that though works councils have worked out well in Germany, they could have turned out to be a substitute for unions," Woodcock said. He said that some U.S. employers tried unsuccessfully in the 1930s to replace the unions with works councils. This experience has given the councils a bad name with American labor.

Rebhan said German unions are forced to expend major efforts to maintain control of works councils. Though they have been successful in this, the road isn't always smooth for the unions. "Sometimes there can be problems because these guys [works council members] become independent barons. A guy says, 'You're going to tell me? I'm elected by the people in my shop.' They can become demagogic, so the unions have to watch it," he said.

Herbert Baker, labor attaché at the U.S. Embassy in Bonn, saw some virtue in the German system of board and works-council co-determination, but felt it isn't something that can be adapted to U.S. usage.

On the positive side, he said, the German system forces managers to factor labor considerations into decision-making at a very early stage. "As soon as an investment is proposed," he said, "labor asks about personnel aspects. The dialogue begins immediately. This is what they teach in any good industrial-relations school in the U.S., but it isn't always done. In Germany, the legal structure forces it to be done."

But Baker contended that the German system, particularly the Works Constitution Act, brings with it a degree of "legislative intervention" that would be completely unacceptable to U.S. business and unions. Besides, he continued, the German Mitbestimmung system was introduced at a unique time in German history. "The complete breakdown in Germany generated conditions that brought in institutions that couldn't have been created otherwise," he said.

"We shouldn't kid ourselves that this is a model for the U.S.," he contended. "Co-determination is an alternative answer in the struggle between capitalism and communism, but not necessarily a transferable idea. You have to work through your own institutions. Germans are proud of Mitbestimmung, but free collective bargaining is equally attractive as a democratic institution, and it has the additional virtue of being more flexible."

The United Auto Workers demand for board representation at Chrysler illustrates how such ideas can hop the Atlantic. Chrysler Corp.'s British subsidiary offered unions in the plant two seats on the company's board as a means of improving worker-management relations. The idea wasn't realized in Britain, but it didn't die. Union President Woodcock said, "We asked, 'If it's good for the British plant, why shouldn't it be good for us?' "

As programs like Mitbestimmung spread through Europe, such incidents probably will multiply. Certainly, many U.S. companies will be exposed intensively to the new parity Mitbestimmung model in Germany. Of the 600 to 650 German companies affected by the new law, some 40 are U.S.-owned.

How does Mitbestimmung work out at these large American-owned companies, and what is ahead under the new law? Interviews with key figures in the process at two of the companies—Ford-Werke AG, a subsidiary of Ford Motor Co., and Adam Opel AG, owned by General Motors Corp.—provided some insights.

Horst Bergemann, personnel director at Ford-Werke, had some misgivings about the new law, centering on increased union representation and the presence of the managerial leitende Angestellte on the labor side. He also thinks there may be quarrels over the position of Arbeitsdirektor, or personnel director, at some companies.

Ford in the past has had a six-member supervisory board consisting of four shareholder representatives and two workers. Limitation of the board to six members had the effect of excluding unionists from outside the company who under the old law could become board members only after the first two labor seats had been filled by company employees.

Under the new law, the board will swell to 20 members. The worker side must include three members nominated by the unions. Bergemann said a special staff might be necessary to lay groundwork for supervisory-board meetings. "The new union men won't know us. They'll need to be prepared," he said. At Ford, these new men will have a voice in a wide range of company affairs, including appointment of the management board, approval of investments above a certain size, and passing on the yearly financial report and dividend rates.

"I hope we'll have reasonable union people" on the supervisory board, he said. Management won't have any influence at all with the unions on whom they appoint, he said, "but the employees will." He said the effect of the new law will be to increase the number of boardroom "arguments and discussions." The union outsiders especially will raise more questions, he said, and there may be arguments over profits and dividends.

In the event of a disputed vote, he said, "the first step will be to try to convince everyone." He added, "But if you can't convince them, then the [chairman's] deciding vote must be cast." He rejected any ideas of changing the company's bylaws to restrict the responsibilities of the board to the legal minimum. The unions know the bylaws, and any attempt to change them would provoke trouble, he indicated.

He said the multinational companies will be "observed very carefully" as they apply the new law.

The representative of the leitenden Angestellen, or managerial white-collar employees, has a tough assignment under the new law, in Bergemann's view. "He is structurally part of management and is in a difficult situation," Bergemann said. "If he follows the capital side every time, he can't be reelected."

Bergemann was personnel manager under the old law, but this title will change to "Arbeitsdirektor" under the new one. He said, "The idea of using the term 'Arbeitsdirektor' in the new law was to create the impression that it was a similar institution to the one in the montan industry. Legally, it isn't."

Nevertheless, he said that in practice it will be "difficult to choose a man as Arbeitsdirektor who is rejected by the unions. It will be somewhat harder to appoint some people as Arbeitsdirektor." If a company appoints as Arbeitsdirektor someone who "by appearance and manner is frustrating" to workers, the man can't live with the new law, according to Bergemann.

He said that in cases where a company nominee for Arbeitsdirektor is disputed by workers, the capital side should overrule the labor side if the opposition is purely "political." But if the labor side has an objective case, then use of the chairman's deciding vote could prove problematical, he said.

Bergemann didn't appear worried about his own position. He said he enjoys a good relationship with workers, though the two sides naturally don't always agree. There is "respect on both sides," he said.

(Bergemann apparently enjoys a good relationship with Heinz Allrup, chairman of the general works council. As I entered Bergemann's office for an interview, he was saying goodbye to Allrup. Allrup jokingly told Bergemann, "Don't tell him anything different from what I said." Then he quipped, "No, tell him something different to emphasize the clash of interests." He banged his fists together to illustrate the point.)

The personnel director said the new bill reflects the powerhunger of the German unions rather than the desires of the workers, who never have given parity board-level participation first priority on their bargaining list. He said he considered the attitude of American unions more reasonable: let the companies make all the profit they want and the unions then get their share of it. The German approach smacks of a union attempt to take over companies, he said.

Whatever his doubts about the wisdom of the new bill, Bergemann appears sold on the works-council system. "We sometimes complain that we aren't so flexible on some things [because of the works council system], but our labor record shows that we've been successful," he said. "The act has forced managers to recognize their responsibilities to people."

Even production experts, who sometimes claim they don't have anything to do with people, must keep workers in mind under the law, he said.

"The law literally says there must be partnership," he said. "That means the company can't ignore the views of people, and workers can't ignore economic realities." The law keeps strikes low by prescribing a "peace obligation." He said the works councils in Germany have more possibilities of "interference" in the company than U.S. unionized workers because of the Works Constitution Act and numerous other labor laws that they help enforce. "This is a piano that the works councils play on," he said. But work goes on despite quarrels. The most recent wildcat strike at Ford had been in 1973.

When agreement can't be reached, disputes go to an arbitrator or to the labor court. "Labor courts tend to be pro-labor," Bergemann said. "That's natural because they were established to protect workers, but they can't ignore the law."

The neutral outsider on arbitration panels often is a labor court judge, Bergemann said. "These people tend to be pro-labor, but their views differ and they can't ignore economic facts."

Ernst Lück is a worker-director on the supervisory board, as well as a member of the works council. Lück, who belongs to the I.G. Metall union, has been on the council since 1959 and has been freed of other duties since 1963. His hopes for increased worker power under the new law are subdued.

For one thing, the leitende Angestellte representative is likely to vote with capital, he said. "It's probably 11 to 9," he said of the new voting configuration. "Under this new law, nothing can happen. Unfortunately."

"One can't expect miracles from the new law," he said. "Co-determination isn't alone-determination. There will always have to be compromises. Even if there were complete equality, we'd still have to agree."

Nevertheless, he does expect the new law will enable workers to get more information about their company and will further the humanization of work. He feels the law will force the Arbeitsdirektor to disclose more information to workers. On past occasions, he said, information has been withheld from the works councils. "We've heard of some things first by jungle drum," he complained.

The information gleaned from supervisory-board meetings

generally has been good, but it comes only four times a year. Secrecy rules forbid the passing of this information to the works council, he notes. Nevertheless, it has been known in the history of the Works Constitution Act that worker-directors have tipped works-council members to potentially fruitful areas for questions at the council meetings with company officials.

Despite the 4 to 2 voting configuration of the board under the old law, worker-directors did make some progress in humanization of work, and this should increase under the new regime, he said. Among their successes at Ford was a project to raise the final assembly line out of a pit that workers found confining. The work involved cost the company "millions," he said.

Lück, who studied balance sheet analysis at an I.G. Metall school, said most boardroom disputes between capital and labor came in connection with approval of company accounts. He said, "We believe that if there is profit, then the worker should get some of it." Worker directors had proposed, so far without success, that each long-time worker be given a free share, either in the German subsidiary (there is at present a miniscule portion of shares in German hands) or in the U.S. company. The capital side has rejected this, and under the 4 to 2 configuration there's nothing to be done.

"When there is no profit, there are no questions," he said. "This year there was a profit."

Lück said worker-directors didn't dispute the need for shareholders to get a fair return on capital. But, he was asked, what is fair?

"What do you get on your savings bank book?" he said. "Four or five percent? Five or six? We won't quarrel with that. If it's 10 to 20, then we must talk about it. If it's 20, 30 or 40 percent, that's too much." He conceded, however, that returns must match the general market level.

Lück welcomed the imminent presence of outside union representatives on the board. "Unions have a better overall view than we do," he said. "We have a view of this plant only." He said this experience will help management to avoid mistakes. He dismissed the argument that outsiders lack the specific knowledge of the auto industry needed to make sound judgments. The outside capital representatives who sit on many companies' boards don't have this knowledge either, he said.

Overall, Lück seemed satisfied with the position of the German worker in the economy.

He said the German worker has "the best security and most rights" of any in the world. "In the U.S., people can be thrown out into the street overnight. That can't happen here." During the auto recession that followed the oil-price increases, he noted, no one at Ford-Werke was fired. Instead the company offered financial incentives to workers to leave. As a result, it was possible to transfer white-collar workers with blue-collar experience back into production jobs. The works council insisted successfully that these men take no pay cut. Later, the pickup in demand for autos allowed these people to start shifting back to their old jobs.

Lück noted with some amusement that foreigners often have trouble understanding the German industrial-relations system. English journalists seeking information sometimes go away baffled. Even Ford people from the U.S. may be puzzled. He said that a one-time Ford-Werke American supervisory-board member on the capital side showed surprise when a worker-director asked him a question about product quality.

Workers understand, said Lück, "that quality sells itself. There's a common interest of management and workers in quality."

Heinz Allrup, the chairman of the general works council, presides over the activities of six local councils. The overall council consists of two representatives from each of the local councils. It operates out of offices in the main Ford administration building. Its office space, supplies and secretaries, by law, are paid for by the company.

The largest of the local councils is the one at the main Cologne plant, which has 27,000 workers. The 41-member council consists of 10 white-collar and 31 blue-collar workers. Two members are women.

Thirty-seven of the 41 are freed from other duties, a greater number than that required by the law, because of a special agreement with Ford. Pay of the freed members is comparable with workers in the departments from which they have been released. If the workers in their department get overtime, the released counterparts get it too.

The co-determination powers of the works council in deciding who should be hired and who promoted, it is sometimes charged, in effect means that German workers have two bosses—the employer and the works council. Allrup didn't argue this point but noted that the council normally gives routine approval to individual management proposals in hiring and promoting.

True, each job applicant must be interviewed by the council prior to hiring, but this normally is just an administrative detail, he said. He named two exceptions, though. The works council might object if it turned out the applicant had a record of theft. Or it might veto the hiring if the company were operating with many men laid off.

Routine approval also would be the rule if a worker wanted to change to a higher-paying job for which a vacancy developed. But he said the council might object if the worker involved were the least qualified of the competitors for the job or if in the judgment of the council the job would endanger his health. "In a case like this, the worker might be sore at the council," he noted.

Bergemann, the personnel director, said the man on the floor doesn't have two bosses, although the man must recognize that the works council does have "some say" in his promotion. But the council recognizes that competence is the decisive criterion for promotion. The council must "argue objectively" if it opposes someone's upward move.

The works council has its fingers in many pies. It "codetermines on kitchen needs," for example. In connection with this duty, the council introduced automated snack dispensers in the factory when it became hard to hire people to push snack carts through the production halls. Council members roam work areas, listening to workers' complaints and making sure working conditions conform to the many legal standards in Germany.

A worker has the legal right to demand to sit at his work if the work can be done sitting, for example. This, Allrup said, is the so-called "Sitzgelegenheit" (opportunity-to-sit) rule laid down in the Work Place Law.

Once a month the overall works council meets with a management-board representative. The economic committee, comprising one man from each council, meets four times yearly with all management-board members for an information exchange. Allrup said the board is generous with facts and figures. He said that if important news sometimes comes instead, as

Lück complained, "by jungle drum," this is only because the management board itself doesn't know about plans that arrive from higher up. Other duties include joint meetings with management on the safety committee.

Among the overall council's biggest accomplishments, Allrup cited the switchover of top skilled workers to monthly from hourly pay and increasing the top reward for accepted employee suggestions to 15,000 marks plus a car from 10,000 marks and a car.

Issues included a demand for a bigger Christmas bonus and elimination of the use of time clocks. The use of time clocks isn't necessary, Allrup contended, because the assembly line imposes its own discipline. When it begins moving in the morning, everyone must be there. If additional monitoring is necessary, this can be done by the foreman, often a union man.

By law, works councils are prevented from calling strikes or slowdowns or using other such tactics. Officially, disputes are resolved by discussion and ultimately by a court or arbitrator. But when the going gets tough, the works councils may use a bit of leverage.

Such an occasion can come after the union has negotiated industry-wide agreements setting increases in the minimum wage. It then falls to works councils in a company that may be paying well above the minimum to ensure that the percentage increase in the minimum also is applied to their higher wages.

"We can't strike," Allrup said. But, we have other Spielchen [little games]." For example? "Management is saying they want more overtime but we"—he cups his ear—"may not be able to hear."

Allrup, and I.G. Metall member, endorses the Mitbestimmung system. He notes that the British unions that had spurned the system "now think there may be something to it." Mitbestimmung means co-responsibility," he concludes.

At Opel in 1976, the company was involved in a dispute with the works council at Rüsselsheim over Christmas bonuses. The dispute and its resolution provide a good example of how the works-council system works.

The argument started at the end of August 1976, when works councils at Rüsselsheim and Bochum plants turned down a management proposal for four extra shifts at each of the plants, to be run in September and October. The works councils based their refusal on management's rejection of the council's proposal, made in the spring, for creation of a special fund to benefit workers temporarily laid off.

The fund would have made up the difference between full pay and the official state compensation for temporarily laid-off workers. Compensation nominally amounts to 68% of normal net pay. The proposal was similar in principle to the supplemental unemployment benefits (SUB) program in effect in some U.S. companies.

The personnel manager, Walter Schlotfeldt, said the situation in Germany wasn't comparable to that in the U.S. because Germany has a "fantastic" system of state compensation for temporarily laid-off workers. He said the 68% net pay figure actually works out to 95% of the net pay of a worker laid off for a week per month, considering that the benefits aren't taxed and that the state and the company take over the employee's contributions to social security. The loss of 5% is "no joke," he said, but it must be remembered that a laid-off worker has fewer expenses than his working counterpart.

At any rate, the company refused to budge on the works councils' demand, with the result that arbitration committees were formed by the two sides in Bochum and Rüsselsheim to resolve the question of the extra shifts. The works council and management representatives at Rüsselsheim weren't able to agree on neutral men for the committee, so a labor court made the choice.

The proceedings resulted in different decisions at Bochum and Rüsselsheim. The Bochum workers were ordered to work the four extra shifts, in return receiving short guarantees against layoffs and firings and certain rights to Christmas-season overtime pay.

The Rüsselsheim decision required workers to work only two special shifts, and there weren't any concessions. But new troubles soon broke out at Rüsselsheim, this time having to do with Christmas bonuses.

The collective-bargaining agreement covering Opel stipulates that companies pay their workers 40% of one month's normal pay as a Christmas bonus. Under separate agreements with the works councils, Opel pays 100%.

In 1976, Opel management agreed for the first time to factor into the computation of Christmas bonuses the pay workers earn on extra shifts. Base period for the computation was to be November 1975 through October 1976. However, the company conditioned the inclusion of the final two months of 1975, during which four extra shifts had been worked, on workers accepting two extra shifts each in September and October 1976. When the Rüsselsheim arbitration committee decided upon only two extra shifts for Rüsselsheim workers, the company changed the base period at Rüsselsheim to January-October 1976. The loss of six extra shifts—four from 1975 and two from 1976—meant a reduction for Rüsselsheim workers of extra-shift Christmas bonus pay to seven hours from nine hours per man. Bochum employees, on the other hand, were to receive their full share, amounting to 9⅓ hours.

The inequality between the two plants rankled workers at Rüsselsheim. Schlotfeldt, the personnel manager, then came up with a new proposal, the keystone of which was the scheduling of two extra shifts in January, restoring of the two hours' pay, as well as guarantees against layoffs and firings and concessions on Christmas-season overtime similar to those at Bochum.

The Rüsselsheim works council agreed, finally ending the dispute. "About time," Schlotfeldt commented happily as he poured coffee for visitors in his office following his meeting with works-council members.

Schlotfeldt said he was "deeply convinced that the Works Constitution Act fosters labor peace at the plant level," in part by forcing management to consider the personnel aspects of each decision. He characterized himself as a "strong defender of free enterprise" but said it's important for management to know how labor will react to company plans. Class war belongs to history, he said. The most recent wildcat strike within the company had been in 1973, when "radical groups" in the plant made demands for cost-of-living pay adjustments, he said.

But a major prerequisite for successful functioning of the system, he said, is that "both management and the works councils believe in the [economic] system and don't want to destroy it." He warned foreigners examining the German system not to assume that it can be transferred successfully to other countries. The works council system fits into a larger scheme of German institutions and might not work in other countries lacking these institutions, he said.

Schlotfeldt rejected suggestions that the information given to German works-council economic committees was perhaps the same type of material U.S. unions could get by reading the newspapers, due to stricter U.S. disclosure requirements. He claimed German workers get more information. The economic committee meets each month with management and gets latest profit, cash flow, and turnover situation reports and predictions, as well as advance notice of price increases.

He said the rigorous requirements on management to give data to workers strengthened the workers' hand in money negotiations. "They aren't forced to inform us," on the other hand, he commented wryly. But he noted that while well-informed workers tend to make bigger demands in good times, they are more willing in bad times to trim their expectations.

Like Bergemann at Ford, Schlotfeldt was less than enthusiastic about the new board-level Mitbestimmung law, which he sees as making management generally more difficult. There is a risk that the increased worker participation will turn the supervisory board into a bargaining unit.

He also expressed fear that the shareholder side of some German companies would compromise with the unions on the selection of management-board members, especially the Arbeitsdirektor. The unions feel that the Arbeitsdirektor should be their man, he said, but a personnel director can be independent only if named by the capital side.

"If I were dependent on the unions, my attitude might change," he said. He said he was young enough now to find a new job if not renamed to his post, but he asked, "How about in 10 years?"

Rudolf Hahn, chairman of the general works council at Opel and a worker-director on the board, welcomes the new bill but, like Lück at Ford, doesn't expect miracles. Hahn noted that the chairman's extra vote and the presence of the leitende Angestellte on the board rule out any true "parity" in connection with the new law.

He hopes that the changes brought by the new law will give workers more information about the company. He also is eager to get the help of outside unionists. (Like Ford, Opel has had only six supervisory board members, meaning that outside unionists have been excluded.) He said, his duties on the works council and supervisory board haven't left him enough time for checking the work of management-board members.

Hahn didn't appear entirely satisfied with the course of supervisory board activities under the old law. He said his feeling was that "too little is decided at the meetings." He had never heard any discussion of investment, for example. The board consists of four Americans shareholder representatives and two German workers. An interpreter is therefore necessary at the meetings.

He said, however, that he was a relatively new member of the board, having joined in April 1975, and had attended only three meetings. He did concede board membership produced valuable information for worker participants.

Meanwhile, the U.S. Chamber of Commerce in Germany, which strongly opposed the original Mitbestimmung bill, said officially that it "can live with" the new bill, though grumblings among members are audible. New U.S. direct investment in Germany, which dipped sharply to 54.5 million marks in the first half of 1975, (equivalent to about $22.8 million at the time), recovered in the first six months of 1976 to 426 million, (equivalent to about $165.5 million at that time), apparently reflecting an easing of earlier fears about Mitbestimmung.

Nevertheless, one source close to the U.S. Chamber wondered whether Germany would remain a powerful magnet for U.S. funds. In the period covered by official statistics, Sept. 1, 1961, through June 30, 1976, the U.S. was the biggest foreign direct investor in Germany with a total of 17.561 billion marks, (equal to $6.822 billion at June 30, 1976, exchange rates), far ahead of the next biggest, Switzerland, with 7.007 billion (equal to $2.722 billion). The source said that U.S. firms would continue "maintenance investment," but that major new outlays were unlikely.

The U.S. freedom from Mitbestimmung seems to be helping to make America a haven for German direct-investment funds. In the first half of 1976, the U.S. was the biggest single recipient of German funds, with 656 million marks, more than double the amount going to the Netherlands, the next most favored country. Representatives of the State of Ohio, who visited Germany in 1976 seeking German investment, told me repeatedly that a major motive of German businessmen seeking to start operations in the U.S. was fear of the socialist trend implicit in the new bill.

Stern Magazine in its April 8, 1976, issue on the U.S. bicentennial, quoted Dieter H. Ambros, of BASF's U.S. subsidiary, as saying he can make more profit in the U.S. with fewer and less educated personnel. "We produce more cheaply." The magazine said this is possible because workers can be hired and fired more quickly. "There are scarcely any contracts. The dismissal notice is 14 days," it commented.

Stern said that German investment in America pays off not only because land and energy are comparatively cheap there but also, as Ambros told the magazine, because the social costs are comparable to those of Germany "prior to the First World War." America is the "praised land of capitalism," he said.

Similar thoughts are expressed by a French business executive, who told The Wall Street Journal that MBA's trained in the U.S. are having a hard time in France, in part because U.S. business schools tend to stress the profit motive above all else. "Thus an MBA may return to France from the U.S., go to work for a French company and announce that the company should move its operations to, say, Hong Kong, because it would be more profitable that way—regardless of the social consequences and the human factors," this unidentified executive said. "This approach simply didn't go over."[4]

Even allowing for the undoubted element of hyperbole contained in both of these statements, it appears the U.S. approach to labor relations may be sharply different from the European.

Germany's Minister of Research and Technology, Hans Matthöfer, is a long-time observer of the U.S. labor scene. He studied economics and sociology at the University of Wisconsin in 1951 and 1952, and served in Washington as a member of the delegation of the Organization for Economic Cooperation and Development from 1957 to 1960. A socialist who rose to political power through service as an I.G. Metall union official, he has kept close tabs on developments in American industrial relations.

In an interview, he discussed Mitbestimmung, making a number of pointed references to the U.S. that may prove thought-provoking and controversial for Americans:

Q. Is Mitbestimmung a particularly German phenomenon? Or can other countries adopt it with success?

A. Well, as far as the reality is concerned, I think it's a particular German phenomenon because you don't have any other country in the world that has introduced not only the concept but also the laws regulating Mitbestimmung like you have in Germany. Since Germans are not different from any other people in the world—different as far as biological substance or intelligence or general reactions are concerned—I think that it is an appropriate arrangement for any other industrial society.

Q. Has Mitbestimmung had a beneficial effect on the German economy? Would German business have had the same success story in any case, under any system of industrial relations?

A. Well, I don't know about the second hypothetical question, but as to the first I believe that Mitbestimmung has had a beneficial effect on the German economy for various reasons. First of all, you have a greater social security. For instance, in mining—and we only have Mitbestimmung as a [true] 50-50 proposition in mining and steel—we have handled the problems of a mining industry diminishing its employment by about 50% without any great social unrest and without any great burden for the individual. This means you have here two eminently reasonable things. You have a 50% participation of workers on the board who did not fight what was economically reasonable, and secondly you have under their influence companies that provide for a scheme that allows the individual ample time and opportunity to adjust to the new situation and recompense him economically for any trouble he may have in changing.

That's one. Second is the impact of co-determination on the style of the struggle of the labor movement. Now, 25 years ago American labor unions were rather condescending when they discussed with us the effectiveness of our methods and theirs. I think that the effectiveness of the German labor movement in increasing its own power, increasing the real standard of living of its members without strikes which have inflicted substantial damage on the economy but guarding the ability to strike has something to do with co-determination. Why? Because in negotiating our people, the labor people, know the real [financial] situation just as management does. And management knows they know. So starting from there, it's much easier to get a realistic agreement. For example, this year the German labor movement has been satisfied with lower wage increases, guarding the real standard of living and only slightly increasing it, because that's the economically indicated thing to do.

A third point: The process of co-determination allows the wisdom, the experience, the professional capability of the employees to be brought into the industrial decision-making process and thereby improves its quality substantially. It increases productivity because a man works better at his job if he's not being pushed around for reasons that he cannot determine but instead believes he can have some kind of influence on the hierachy. And it changes the style of the hierarchy. Now that we are going to have the nearly 50-50 arrangement in all companies with more than 2,000 members, there will be labor people on board against whom there will be no appointment of Vorstand members. This [management-board membership] is of course the important jump in the life of a manager. This is where the big money is. Until then, it's more or less chicken feed by comparison. At this point, he knows there will be people who remember what he did when he was on the way up. And people who can say 'Come on, bring us another guy, not him.' And the managers change their attitude. They deal with their people in a different fashion, because they know they'll need them at a particularly important point in their career. This changes the whole atmosphere.

Q. Do you think that this applies even though it isn't quite 50-50?

A. Oh, yes. You see, the fact is that you cannot have decisions like that very many times against the other side. And there have been very, very few really conflict situations, because before the meeting starts the two sides have found an arrangement in the common interest. And in this type of [atmosphere], if the other side says, 'No, not him, find someone else,' he won't even be presented. No man is so good as to justify antagonizing a whole faction that has nearly 50% of the decision-making power.

Q. Do you see any evidence that the parity Mitbestimmung in the montan industry has been more effective for the worker and for the economy than the one-third Mitbestimmung in the other industries?

A. First of all, steel and coal are particular industries. You must know the industry to know the importance of Mitbestimmung for the workers. This has been an industry where in the early years of the 20th century foreign workers—Poles, Italians—had been disciplined by nearly military organization to industrial effectiveness. This way of treating people persisted. It kind of creates a tradition. Mitbestimmung broke this tradition. Workers became important. Management knew they were important. Older people remember and tell their sons. This is one of the sources of the strength of the Social Democratic Party in the Rhine-Ruhr area—that we changed the climate in the working place in favor of the worker. We did not introduce a social machine that didn't care for the individual, but we got co-determination. Well, of course, it's bureaucratic, but somehow you have to watch out for your people if they have to elect you and keep voting for you. And you do this, you get in the habit of listening to the individual and caring for him.

As far as the information of co-determination is concerned, I don't think it makes a great deal of difference whether you have one-third or half. You get the information and that's it. This one-third form has been much more effective than most people think, because of this [capital] attitude that you cannot always vote against labor. So even this one-third has always been more powerful than either side would admit. Neither had an interest in explaining why it took the other side into consideration.

Q. Nonetheless, you feel that the jump from one-third to nearly one-half was needed?

A. Yes, it's needed, and of course I think this latest law is just one step. Now we have to think about the next. That's why I've been taking all this philosphically. It's just one more step in the direction of the democratization of industry.

Q. What's the next one?

A. First, we've got a couple of years of implementing this law. Then I think there should be more co-determination for the individual worker on the job, which is a different law—the Works Constitution Act. We improved this law in 1972. Maybe 1982 is a good year to have another look at this particular law. We should keep increasing the rights of the man on the job, enlarge his area of self-determination and see what happens. We should be very careful about it, but my general philosophy is that the more qualified a working force is, the more you get a type of organization of groups that are in themselves democratically organized, cooperating with each other. That is, you are losing more and more the hierarchy concept of management. Let's say the information function becomes more and more important in the talent mix of a manager. He must be able to inform, to convince and to organize not subordinates but people who cooperate with him because they consider it to be in the common interest. And I think that Mitbestimmung fits exactly into the historical tendency of development of higher and higher qualification in the industrial and administrative processes.

Q. You suggest that the next change should be in the Works Constitution Act. What is your position on the union demand that true voting parity on the board should be the next step?

A. I'm for parity. If the political relationship permits parity, I'll introduce it the next morning. But I don't see this. Not in 1980 and not till 1984—when you [might] get an absolute majority of Social Democrats, who are the only ones who want this.

Q. Does the union movement want to stop at parity or does it want to go onto something more than parity?

A. Well, the DGB [labor federation] wants to stop at parity, according to their program. I don't think you should say there is any end to the process of democratization. Why should you limit yourself? But it isn't a problem of present-day policy.

Q. If you get to parity and beyond, do you think that the function of the shareholder as a financing instrument will be diminished?

A. Not as a financing instrument. I mean you have today generally speaking two types of financing. You have stocks and bonds. If you buy a bond, you have no power of decision. You have the right to get your money back for your bond and you have the right to a fair interest rate. Of course, you can imagine a situation—which at present we do not have politically in Germany—where the rights of the stockholder are changing. Piece by piece, the people who do the work in the organization get more and more influence and those who just do the outside financing get less influence. I mean theoretically you can construct a model of development in this direction. This isn't present-day policy in Germany, though.

Q. Has Mitbestimmung been a hindrance to the introduction of technological change?

A. No, you see, in 1950-51, when there was a debate, people who were against co-determination argued the following: they said, look, what does a worker have? He has his job. What does technological progress do? It abolishes jobs. So if workers are in an influential position, they will not vote for technological progress because it takes away the only thing they have, which is their jobs. Now, this is an argument that belongs in the trash can of history. We have had co-determination in the steel industry for 30 years. If you look at the technological breakthroughs in the steel industry—the oxygen process, direct reduction, continuous casting, substantial improvement in the blast-furnace process—these were invented and adopted first either in the co-determined German steel industry or in the socialized Austrian steel industry. The oxygen process is the most important because it did away with the open hearth. It improved steel quality. It accelerated the possibility of making good steel by magnitudes. All this we did. Not the American steel industry, which has great amounts of capital, which deals with unions who are against co-determination, which is free of the fetters of all the things that we impose on our companies. The technological progress was ours. And we can prove it. We have history on our side to show it.

Q. Why is it that workers have acted in a way different from that predicted in 1950?

A. Because we are reasonable people. That's all. The Young Socialists in Germany have a slogan. It says: 'Socialism because it's reasonable.' If you treat people right, they'll do their job right. They'll listen to arguments. If jobs are being abolished, the worker will only fight it if you fire him. If he is sure he has full employment, that he can upgrade himself by instruction and getting paid during instruction, that he has enormous social security, and even if he gets unemployed he gets 68% of his net pay, plus child allowance and rent allowance, so that he hardly loses any money, then the prospect of losing a job loses its terror. He can look at this more reasonably. Of course, people realize that if you want to increase their standard of living, then you have to have technological progress. As someone who has been intimately connected with the American scene for about 30 years now, it was for me a proud day when VW decided to put a plant into that low-wage country, the U.S., when they proved that in fact our wages were higher than the wages in Pennsylvania.

In Germany, where you pack 62 million people in an area less than the size of the state of Oregon, where we have to import more than 95% of our iron and our oil, where we have nothing but our coal—which is very expensive—and achieve this standard of living, I think that's good performance, and it has something to do with social security and co-determination and equal opportunity in education.

Q. Who has it better, the American worker with his collective bargaining rights, or the German worker with the rights that he gets through Mitbestimmung?

A. This is a question that you can't answer. The U.S. is a richer country. It is a country of enormous riches. And the question is: What could the standard of living of the American worker be if this country were organized in reasonable fashion? Not having to fight for a job and not having to have featherbedding? You have enormous losses. First, you have the luxury of high unemployment. This leads the worker to fight for his job with all means, which diminishes productivity from what it could be by at least 20%, at least of skilled workers, who do not cross trade lines, for example. I wrote an essay once about the make-work strategies of the American labor movement. You fight for all this with strikes. And if you add all this together, you get every year a couple of percentage points of loss in growth which adds up over the years to 20, 30, 40, even 50% that you might live better if you had organized your industrial lives reasonably. I think our performance in this country with no natural resources except coal shows that co-determination is a good thing.

Q. If you were to place Mitbestimmung somewhere on a scale between unrestrained capitalism and communism, where would you fit it in? Can you do that?

A. No, I have an idea of a society that I want to reach—a society full of freedom, democratic in all possible aspects, where everybody has an equal chance to develop his capabilities, his talents. It is full of social security. People live internally at peace and at peace with their neighbors and fulfill their duties of solidarity with the hungry people of the world. In order to achieve this type of society, I think that Mitbestimmung or co-determination is an important tool. It's an integral part of the strategy, and I couldn't reach what I want without people gradually adjusting themselves and learning how to run their own economic lives.

Co-Determination: Benefits & Limitations

Mitbestimmung should be judged both as an ideology and as a functioning system.

The ideology of co-determination is likely to find wide, although not universal, appeal. It starts with the assumption that labor and capital are equally important to production and therefore should be given equal voices in running major companies.

The need for compromise arising from the parity of labor and capital means that labor is forced constantly to face economic realities, much as it might like to ignore them, while capital is compelled to draw humanistic considerations constantly into its decisions, although its basic tendency is to seek only the highest possible return.

Mitbestimmung legislation giving workers wide powers through participation on the board and through works-council activities represents formal acknowledgement by society of the legitimacy of workers' claims on the company—a legitimacy that isn't always reflected in systems relying solely on collective bargaining. In collective bargaining, the worker is an independent agent, outside the company, who sells his services to the company. Under Mitbestimmung, the worker is as much a part of the company as the shareholder is.

Co-determination isn't intended to end the company's ability to give orders to employees. The system is intended only to ensure that the company's authority receives "democratic legitimation" through the consent of the employees.

There is a certain appearance of inevitability about an ideology that seeks to spread democracy.

But, aside from ideology, what about results? Germany is rich. It is virtually without Communists. It has one of the lowest strike rates among major Western industrialized nations. Its unions, unlike those in Britain and France, aren't driven by the idea of nationalizing industries.

Proving a causal link between Mitbestimmung and Germany's enviable position would be difficult. One can at least say that Mitbestimmung hasn't prevented Germany's rise from the ashes of World War II to a position of economic leadership and increasing political influence.

Moreover, there is little doubt that Germany's low strike rate has contributed to the country's wealth. It is reasonable to assume that the institutionalized processes of communication and accommodation between capital and labor that are promoted by Mitbestimmung have contributed to labor peace.

It isn't hard to explain the dearth of Communists and the coolness of labor toward nationalization in terms of Mitbestimmung's principles. To a large extent the spread of communist ideology and nationalization sentiment among workers elsewhere reflects a sense of frustration and impotence among the work force, a feeling that the powers who run major corporations ignore the working man in their decisions, that these powers must be replaced by administrators subject to popular control.

Mitbestimmung tends to reduce frustration and impotence among workers by giving them steady access to and influence on company power centers. It gives them the ability to help determine their own fates. Responsible conduct is apt to be the result.

There is a price. Mitbestimmung is "inefficient" in the sense that a democracy is less efficient than a military government. Mitbestimmung is "bureaucratic," admitted Hans Matthöfer, a backer of the system. Said Peter Frerk, VW personnel chief, also a proponent, "You have to talk to everyone and convince people. There are always questions, questions, questions."

However successful it may be in Germany, Mitbestimmung can't necessarily be transferred intact to other countries. For one thing, West Germany's remarkably stable labor-capital relationship isn't matched in many other countries. Another reason: Mitbestimmung is strong medicine. Applied at the end of a disastrous war to a country emerging from a dictatorship, it helped revive democratic forces. Applied too fast to an already highly democratic society, it conceivably could prove overstimulative.

In any case, it should be noted that even Germany didn't go over to its system of near-parity Mitbestimmung on a national basis until it had tested parity co-determination in the coal and steel sectors and had experimented with one-third co-determination elsewhere for about a quarter of a century.

Although a go-slow approach probably is prudent, this principle isn't being following in all cases. British unions, for example, are demanding instant parity Mitbestimmung.

Whatever its potential hazards and opportunities, Mitbestimmung is a firmly established European trend. This trend in the past has been relatively little noticed in the U.S., but America is beginning to pay more attention.

Appendix

ACT ON CO-DETERMINATION BY JOBHOLDERS (Co-Determination Act) of May 4, 1976 (Federal Law Gazette I p. 1153)

PART ONE
Scope of Application

Article 1
Enterprises falling under this act

(1) Jobholders have the right of co-determination under this act in enterprises which

1. are legally constituted and operated as a joint stock company ["Aktiengesellschaft"], a partnership based on shares ["Kommanditgesellschaft auf Aktien"], a company in the form of a "Gewerkschaft" under mining statutes ["bergrechtliche Gewerkschaft mit eigener Rechtspersönlichkeit"] or a profit-oriented economic cooperative ["Erwerbs- und Wirtschaftsgenossenschaft"], and which
2. as a rule, employ more than 2,000 jobholders.

(2) This act does not apply to co-determination in the organs of enterprises in which jobholders have a co-determination right according to

1. the Act on Co-determination by Jobholders in the Supervisory and Management Boards of Mining, Iron and Steel Industry Enterprises of May 21, 1951 (Federal Law Gazette I p. 347)—Mining, Iron and Steel Industry Co-determination Act ["Montanmitbestimmungsgesetz"]—last amended by the Introductory Act to the Joint Stock Company Act ["Aktiengesetz"] of September 6, 1965 (Federal Law Gazette I p. 1185), or
2. the Supplementary Act to the Act on Co-determination by Jobholders in the Supervisory and Management Boards of Mining, Iron and Steel Industry Enterprises of August 7, 1956 (Federal Law Gazette I p. 707)—Co-determination Sup-

plementary Act ["Mitbestimmungsergänzungsgesetz"]—, last amended by the Amendment Act to the Supplementary Act to the Act on Co-Determination by Jobholders in the Supervisory and Management Boards of Mining, Iron and Steel Industry Enterprises of April 27, 1967 (Federal Law Gazette I p. 505).

(3) The representation of jobholders in the supervisory boards of enterprises whose jobholders do not have the right of co-determination, as defined in the acts referred to in Section 1 or Section 2, is regulated by the provisions of the Works Constitution Act ["Betriebsverfassungsgesetz"] of 1952 (Federal Law Gazette I p. 681), last amended by the Works Constitution Act of January 15, 1972 (Federal Law Gazette I p. 13).

(4) This act does not apply to enterprises which directly and predominantly serve

1. political, party political, religious, charitable, educational, scientific or artistic purposes, or
2. the purposes of reporting or free expression of opinion to which Article 5, Section 1, Sentence 2 of the Basic Law ["Grundgesetz" or federal constitution] applies.

This act may not be applied to religious associations and their charitable and educational institutions, irrespective of their legal form.

Article 2
Shareholders

Shareholders within the meaning of this act are, according to the individual legal form of the enterprises referred to in Art. 1, Section 1, No. 1: shareholders, partners, "Gewerken" [shareholders in an enterprise organized as a "Gewerkschaft" under mining statutes], or "Genossen" [members of a profit-oriented economic cooperative.]

Article 3
Jobholders

(1) Jobholders within the meaning of this act are wage-earning workers and salaried employes ["Arbeiter" and "Angestellte," i.e., blue-collar workers and white-collar employees].

The persons defined in Art. 5, Section 2, of the Works Constitution Act are not jobholders within the meaning of this act.

(2) Blue-collar workers within the meaning of this act are the jobholders defined in Art. 6, Section 1, of the Works Constitution Act.

(3) White-collar employees within the meaning of this act are

1. the white-collar employees defined in Art. 6, Section 2, of the Works Constitution Act, with the exception of white-collar employees with managerial responsibility ["leitende Angestellte" or managerial white-collar employees] as defined in Art. 5, Section 3, of the Works Constitution Act,
2. managerial white-collar employees as defined in Art. 5, Section 3, of the Works Constitution Act.

Article 4
Limited partnership

(1) If an enterprise defined in Art. 1, Section 1, No. 1, is a personally liable partner of a limited partnership, and if the majority of the limited partners of this limited partnership—computed according to the majority of the shares or votes—also holds the majority of the shares or votes in the company of the personally liable partner, the jobholders of the limited partnership are deemed to be jobholders of the personally liable partner, unless the personally liable partner has its own business employing, as a rule, more than 500 jobholders. If the limited partnership is the personally liable partner of another limited partnership, its jobholders also are deemed to be employees of the enterprise specified in Art. 1, Section 1, No. 1. This applies accordingly if the chain of limited partnerships is continued in this manner.

(2) The enterprise [the personally liable partner] cannot be excluded from management of the limited partnership.

Article 5
Groups of Companies

(1) If an enterprise defined in Art. 1, Section 1, No. 1, is the controlling company of a group (Art. 18, Section 1 of the Joint

Stock Company Act), then, in applying this act to the controlling company, the jobholders of member companies of the group are deemed to be jobholders of the controlling company. This also applies to jobholders of an enterprise, as defined in Art. 1, Section 1, No. 1, which is the personally liable partner of a dependent company (Art. 18, Section 1 of the Joint Stock Company Act) organized as a limited partnership.

(2) If a limited partnership—whose jobholders are deemed to be jobholders of the personally liable partner in applying this act to the personally liable partner according to Art. 4, Section 1—is the controlling company in a group (Art. 18, Section 1 of the Joint Stock Company Act), then, in applying this act to the personally liable partner of the limited partnership, the jobholders of member companies of the group are deemed to be employees of the personally liable partner. Section 1, Sentence 2, and Art. 4, Section 2, apply accordingly.

(3) Where member companies in a group are controlled by an enterprise other than one defined in Section 1 or 2, but where the group management controls other member companies of the group via one or several enterprises defined in Section 1 or 2, then, in applying this act, the controlling companies are deemed to be those, as defined in Section 1 or 2, which are closest to the group management and through which the controlling company exerts its power of control.

PART TWO
SUPERVISORY BOARD

First Division
Formation and Composition

Article 6
Basic principle

(1) Companies defined in Art. 1, Section 1, will form a supervisory board insofar as this does not already follow from other legal provisions.

(2) The formation and composition of the supervisory board and the appointment and dismissal of its members are regulated by Articles 7 to 24 of this act, and, insofar as this does not

already follow from other legal provisions, by Art. 96, Section 2, Articles 97 to 101, Sections 1 and 3 and Articles 102 to 106 of the Joint Stock Company Act; with the proviso that a "Prokurist" [an authorized manager with wide legal powers to act on behalf of a company] is only ineligible for election as a supervisory board member representing jobholders if he is directly subordinate to the organ which is entitled to represent the company legally, and if he is authorized to act on the entire range of business with which the organ deals. Other legal regulations and provisions of the bylaws (articles of association, statute) regarding the composition of the supervisory board and the appointment and dismissal of its members remain unaffected, insofar as they do not contradict provisions of this act.

(3) Articles 100, 101, Sections 1 and 3, and Articles 103 and 106 of the Joint Stock Company Act do not apply to profit-oriented economic cooperatives. Art. 9, Section 2 of the Act on Profit-oriented Economic Cooperatives does not apply to jobholder supervisory board members.

Article 7
Composition of the Supervisory Board

(1) The supervisory board of an enterprise with, as a rule,

1. not more than 10,000 jobholders, is composed of six representatives each of the shareholders and jobholders;
2. more than 10,000 but no more than 20,000 jobholders, is composed of eight representatives each of the shareholders and the jobholders;
3. more than 20,000 jobholders, is composed of 10 representatives each of the shareholders and jobholders.

In the case of enterprises defined in Sentence 1, No. 1, the bylaws (articles of association, statute) may determine that Sentence 1, No. 2 or 3, applies. In the case of enterprises defined in Sentence 1, No. 2, the bylaws (articles of association, statute) may determine that Sentence 1, No. 3, applies.

(2) The jobholder supervisory-board members must include

1. in a supervisory board with six jobholder members: four jobholders of the enterprise and two trade-union representatives;

2. in a supervisory board with eight jobholder members: six jobholders of the enterprise and two trade-union representatives;
3. in a supervisory board with ten jobholder members: seven jobholders of the enterprise and three trade-union representatives.

(3) The jobholders of the enterprise referred to in Section 2 must have completed their 18th year of life, have been employed by the enterprise for one year and must satisfy the other eligibility criteria contained in Art. 8 of the Works Constitution Act.

(4) The trade unions referred to in Section 2 must be represented in the enterprise itself, or in another enterprise whose jobholders participate according to this act in the election of supervisory-board members of the enterprise.

Second Division
Appointment of Supervisory-Board Members

First Subdivision
Shareholder Supervisory Board Members

Article 8

(1) Shareholder supervisory board members are appointed by the organ empowered by law, bylaws, articles of partnership or statute to elect members of the supervisory board [electoral body], and, insofar as legal provisions do not contradict them, according to the bylaws, articles of partnership or statute.

(2) Art. 101, Section 2, of the Joint Stock Company Act remains unaffected.

Second Subdivision
Jobholder Supervisory-Board Members, Basic Principle

Article 9

(1) The jobholder supervisory-board members (Art. 7, Section 2) of an enterprise with, as a rule, more than 8,000 jobholders, are elected by electors ["Wahlmänner"], insofar as vote-entitled jobholders do not decide on direct elections.

(2) Jobholder supervisory-board members (Art. 7, Section 2) of an enterprise with, as a rule, no more than 8,000 jobholders, are elected in direct elections, insofar as vote-entitled jobholders do not decide on elections through electors.

(3) In order to vote on whether the election should be carried out through electors or directly, an application signed by one-twentieth of the vote-entitled jobholders of an enterprise is required. The vote is secret. A decision under Section 1 or 2 can be taken only if at least half of the vote-entitled jobholders take part and only with the majority of the votes cast.

Third Subdivision
Election of Jobholder Supervisory-Board Members Through Electors

Article 10
Election of Electors

(1) In each facility ["Betrieb"] of the enterprise, the blue-collar workers (Art. 3, Section 2) and the white-collar employees (Art. 3, Section 3) shall elect their electors in separate and secret elections, based on the principle of election by proportional representation. Art. 4 of the Works Constitution Act shall apply to branches and separate departments of the facility, as shall also arrangements made under Art. 3, Section 1, No. 3 of the Works Constitution Act in collective agreements in connection with the relationship of branches and separate departments to the facility.

(2) Deviating from Section 1, deputies will be elected by joint ballot if vote-entitled blue-collar workers and white-collar employees of the enterprise so decide in separate, secret votes. Decisions in terms of Sentence 1 can be taken only on application of one-twentieth of the vote-entitled members of both groups, with at least half participating and only with a majority of votes cast in both groups.

(3) Those entitled to participate in the election of electors are jobholders of the enterprise who have completed their 18th year of life.

(4) Those eligible for election as electors are the jobholders

defined in Section 3, who must also fulfil the other eligibility criteria defined in Art. 8 of the Works Constitution Act.

(5) If only one list of candidates is submitted in a ballot, then the jobholders listed in it are deemed to be elected in the stated sequence. Art. 11, Section 2, applies.

Article 11
Computation of the Number of Electors

(1) There will be one elector for every 60 vote-entitled jobholders in every facility. If the computation in terms of Sentence 1 should cause one group in a plant to be represented by more than

1. 30 electors, then the number of electors to be elected is reduced to one half; these electors receive two ballots each;
2. 90 electors, then the number of electors to be elected is reduced to one third; these electors receive three ballots each;
3. 150 electors, then the number of electors to be elected is reduced to one quarter; these electors receive four ballots each.

In computing the number of electors, fractions of a number are counted fully if they amount to at least half of the full number.

(2) The blue-collar workers and white-collar employees must be represented among the electors in every facility according to their numerical proportion. Among the electors of the white-collar employees, the white-collar employees defined in Art. 3, Section 3, No. 1 and the managerial white-collar employees must be represented according to their numerical proportions. If in a facility at least nine electors are to be elected, then there must be at least one elector each for the blue-collar workers, white-collar employees defined in Art. 3, Section 3, No. 1, and the managerial white-collar employees; this does not apply insofar as in the facility there are no more than five vote-entitled blue-collar workers, white-collar employees defined in Art. 3, Section 3, No. 1, or managerial white-collar employees. Insofar as the blue-collar workers, the white-collar employees defined in Art. 3, Section 3, No. 1, and the managerial white-collar employees are entitled to electors only according to Sen-

tence 3, the number of electors in the facility computed under Section 1 increases accordingly.

(3) Insofar as according to section 2 the blue-collar workers, white-collar employees defined in Art. 3, Section 3, No. 1, and managerial white-collar employees in a facility are not represented by at least one elector each, these are considered, for the purposes of electing electors, to be jobholders in the facility of the head office of the enterprise. Insofar as, according to Section 2 and Sentence 1, the blue-collar workers, the white-collar employees defined in Art. 3, Section 3, No. 1 and the managerial white-collar employees in the head office plant are not apportioned at least one elector each in the facility of the head office, they are considered for the purposes of electing electors to be jobholders of that facility of the enterprise which has the greatest number of vote-entitled jobholders.

(4) If there is no elector apportioned to a particular facility, Section 3 applies accordingly.

(5) The status of an elector as a representative of the blue-collar workers or the white-collar employees remains unchanged if he changes group membership. Sentence 1 applies accordingly if a white-collar elector changes his status as a white-collar employee defined in Art. 3, Section 3, No. 1, or as a managerial white-collar employee.

Article 12
Candidate Lists for Election of Electors

(1) Vote-entitled jobholders in the facility may submit candidate lists for the election of electors. Every candidate list must be signed in the case of electors of

1. vote-entitled blue-collar workers: by one tenth or 100 of the vote-entitled workers in the facility,
2. the white-collar employees who are apportioned to the white-collar employees defined in Art. 3, Section 3, No. 1: by one tenth or 100 of the vote-entitled white-collar employees defined in Art. 3, Section 3, No. 1,
3. the white-collar employees who are apportioned to the man-

agerial white-collar employees: by one tenth or 100 of the managerial white-collar employees.

(2) Every list should contain at least twice as many candidates as the number of electors to be elected.

Article 13
Term of Office of the electors

(1) The electors are elected for a period that corresponds to the term of office of the supervisory board members whom they elect. They assume the duties and rights assigned them under the provisions of this act until the process of holding new elections for jobholder supervisory board members has been started.

(2) In the cases referred to in Art. 9, Section 1, the term of office of electors ends if:

1. vote-entitled jobholders according to Art. 9, Section 1, decide on direct election;
2. the enterprise no longer fulfills the preconditions for applying Art. 9, Section 1—unless vote-entitled jobholders decide that the term of office should continue until the time mentioned in Section 1; Art. 9, Section 3 applies accordingly.

(3) In the cases referred to in Art. 9, Section 2, the term of office of electors ends if the vote-entitled jobholders decide on direct elections; Art. 9, Section 3 applies.

(4) Deviating from Section 1, the term of office of electors in a facility ends if—after the entry into office of all the substitutes on the candidate list that included the electors to be replaced—the total number of electors in the facility has fallen below the number prescribed for that plant at the time of their election.

Article 14
Premature termination of the term of office or indisposition of electors

(1) An elector's term of office ends before the time stipulated in Art. 13

1. if he resigns his office,

2. if he is no longer employed in the facility where he is an elector,
3. through loss of eligibility.

(2) Should an elector's term of office end prematurely or should he be prevented from carrying out his functions, a substitute takes his place. The substitutes are drawn in the listed sequence from the non-elected candidates on the lists that included the electors who are to be replaced.

Article 15
Election of Jobholder Supervisory-Board Members Belonging to the Enterprise

(1) The electors elect the supervisory-board members who must be jobholders of the enterprise in terms of Art. 7, Section 2, by secret ballot and according to the principles of election by proportional representation, for the period prescribed in the law or in the bylaws (in the articles of partnership, in the statute) for the supervisory-board members who are to be elected by the electoral body of the shareholders.

(2) The supervisory-board members to be elected under Section 1 must comprise blue-collar workers and white-collar employees according to their numerical proportion in the enterprise. White-collar supervisory-board members must include white-collar employees defined in Art. 3, Section 3, No. 1, and managerial white-collar employees, according to their numerical proportions. The supervisory board must include at least one blue-collar worker, one white-collar employee defined in Art. 3, Section 3, No. 1, and one managerial white-collar employee.

(3) Blue-collar supervisory-board members are elected by the worker electors, white-collar supervisory board members by the white-collar employee electors. Deviating from Sentence 1, supervisory board members are elected by joint ballot if the blue-collar electors and the white-collar electors so decide in separate, secret votes. Art. 10, Section 2, Sentence 2 applies accordingly.

(4) The election is conducted on the basis of lists of nominated candidates. Each list of candidates for

1. blue-collar worker supervisory board members must be signed by one-fifth or 100 of the vote-entitled blue-collar workers in the enterprise;
2. white-collar employee supervisory board members who represent the white-collar employees defined in Art. 3, Section 3, No. 1, must be signed by one-fifth or 100 of the vote-entitled white-collar employees in the enterprise as defined in Art. 3, Section 3, No. 1;
3. white-collar employee supervisory-board members who represent the managerial white-collar employees is decided by the vote-entitled managerial white-collar employees by vote on the basis of proposals. Each proposal must be signed by one-twentieth or 50 of the vote-entitled managerial white-collar employees. The decision is made by secret ballot on the basis of the majority of the votes cast. Insofar as the number of candidates prescribed in Section 5, Sentence 3, is not approved by a majority, a second ballot takes place at which new proposals may be put to the vote. After the second ballot, as many candidates as fell short of the number prescribed in Section 5, Sentence 3, after the first ballot may be included in the list in the priority of the number of votes they received. In the voting, each managerial white-collar employee has the same number of ballots as the number of candidates this group must nominate for the candidate list according to Section 5, Sentence 3.

(5) Deviating from Section 1, majority vote election takes place insofar as, according to Section 2, the supervisory board must include only one blue-collar worker, one white-collar employee defined in Art. 3, Section 3, No. 1 or one managerial white-collar employee. Election by majority vote also takes place insofar as only one candidate list is submitted for

1. the blue-collar worker supervisory board members,
2. the white-collar employee supervisory-board members representing the white-collar employees defined in Art. 3, Section 3, No. 1,
3. the white-collar employee supervisory-board members representing the managerial white-collar employees.

Insofar as majority vote election takes place in terms of Sentence 2, the list must contain twice as many candidates as the number of supervisory-board members apportioned among the blue-collar workers, the white-collar employees defined in Art. 3, Section 3, No. 1 or the managerial white-collar employees.

Article 16
Election of Trade Union Supervisory Board Representatives

(1) Supervisory-board members who are union representatives in terms of Art. 7, Section 2, are elected by the electors by joint, secret ballot, according to the principle of proportional representation, for the period determined in Art. 15, Section 1.

(2) The election is based on lists of candidates submitted by unions represented in the enterprise itself, or in another enterprise whose jobholders participate in electing supervisory-board members according to this act. Deviating from Section 1, majority vote election takes place if only one candidate list is submitted. In such a case, the list must contain at least twice as many candidates as the number of union representatives to be elected to the supervisory board.

Article 17
Substitute Members

(1) In every list of candidates, a substitute member of the supervisory board may be proposed together with every candidate on the list. Only a blue-collar worker, only a white-collar employee defined in Art. 3, Section 3, No. 1, and only a managerial white-collar employee may be proposed as a substitute member for every candidate who is respectively a blue-collar worker, a white-collar employee defined in Art. 3, Section 3, No. 1, and a managerial white-collar employee. A candidate may not simultaneously be proposed as a substitute member.

(2) If a candidate is elected as a supervisory-board member, the substitute member proposed along with him is also elected.

Fourth Subdivision
Direct Election of Jobholder Supervisory-Board Members

Article 18

If the jobholder supervisory-board members are to be elected directly in terms of Art. 9, jobholders of the enterprise who have completed their 18th year of life are entitled to vote. Articles 15 to 17 apply to the election, with the proviso that:

1. Vote-entitled blue-collar workers of the enterprise take the place of blue-collar electors.
2. Vote-entitled white-collar employees of the enterprise take the place of white-collar electors.

Fifth Subdivision
Further Provisions Regarding the Election Process and the Appointment and Dismissal of Supervisory-Board Members

Article 19
Publication of the Names of Supervisory-Board Members

Immediately after the members and substitute members of the supervisory board are appointed, the organ which is the legal representative of the enterprise must make their names known by posting them for two weeks in the facilities of the enterprise and by publishing them in the Federal Gazette. If jobholders of another enterprise take part in the election of supervisory-board members of the enterprise, the organ that is the legal representative of the other enterprise is additionally required to post the names in its facilities.

Article 20
Safeguarding Elections and Costs of Elections

(1) No person may obstruct the elections according to Articles 10, 15, 16 and 18. In particular, no person may be restrained in the exercise of his active and passive voting rights.

(2) No person may influence the elections by causing or threatening to cause disadvantage or by granting or promising advantages.

(3) The enterprise bears the cost of the election. Loss of working time that is essential for the exercise of voting rights or for election committee activities does not entitle the employer to reduce wages.

Article 21
Contesting the Election of Electors

(1) The election of electors in a facility may be contested in a labor court if essential provisions regarding voting rights, eligibility or the electoral process have been infringed and no redress has been made, excepting if the infringement could not have changed or influenced the election result.

(2) The following are entitled to contest an election:

1. at least three vote-entitled jobholders of the enterprise,
2. the works council,
3. the organ that is the legal representative of the enterprise.

An election may be contested only within a period of two weeks from the day on which it was announced.

Article 22
Contesting the Election of Jobholder Supervisory-Board Members

(1) The election of a jobholder supervisory-board member or a substitute member may be contested in a labor court if essential provisions regarding voting rights, eligibility or the election process have been infringed and no redress has been made, excepting if the infringement could not have changed or influenced the election result.

(2) The following are entitled to contest an election result:

1. at least three vote-entitled jobholders of the enterprise,
2. the general works council of the enterprise or, if there is only

one works council in the enterprise, the works council; equally, if the enterprise is the controlling company of a group, the group works council, insofar as it exists,

3. the general works council of another enterprise whose jobholders participate in the election of supervisory board members of the enterprise according to this act; or the works council, if there is only one works council in the enterprise,
4. any trade union entitled to make nominations in terms of Art. 16, Section 2.
5. the organ that is the legal representative of the enterprise.

An election may be contested only within a period of two weeks after the day on which it was published in the Federal Gazette.

Article 23
Removal of Jobholder Supervisory-Board Members

(1) A jobholder supervisory-board member may be recalled on application before his term of office expires. Those entitled to apply for removal are, in the case of a

1. supervisory-board member of the blue-collar workers: three-quarters of the vote-entitled blue-collar workers,
2. supervisory board member of the white-collar employees who is apportioned to the white-collar employees defined in Art. 3, Section 3, No. 1: three-quarters of the vote-entitled white-collar employees defined in Art. 3, Section 3, No. 1,
3. supervisory-board member of the white-collar employees who is apportioned to the managerial white-collar employees: three-quarters of the vote-entitled managerial white-collar employees,
4. supervisory-board member, who is a representative of a trade union according to Art. 7, Section 2: the union that proposed the member.

(2) A supervisory-board member elected by electors in separate elections (Art. 15, Section 3, Sentence 1) is removed through the decision of electors of his group. A supervisory-board member elected by electors in joint elections (Art. 15, Section 3, Sentence 2) is removed through the decision of the elec-

tors. Decisions according to Sentences 1 and 2 are made in secret votes; they require a majority of three-quarters of the votes cast.

(3) A supervisory-board member elected directly by the jobholders of one group is removed through the decision of the vote-entitled jobholders of this group. A supervisory-board member elected directly in a joint election by the jobholders is removed through the decision of the vote-entitled jobholders. Decisions according to Sentence 1 and 2 are taken in secret, direct votes; they require a majority of three quarters of the votes cast.

(4) Sections 1 to 3 shall apply accordingly for the removal of substitute members.

Article 24
Loss of Eligibility and Changes in the Group Membership of Supervisory-Board Members Who Belong to the Enterprise

(1) If a supervisory-board member who must—according to Art. 7, Section 2—be a jobholder of the enterprise, loses his eligibility, his office expires.

(2) A change in group membership of a blue-collar worker or white-collar employee supervisory-board member does not cause his office to expire. Sentence 1 shall apply accordingly if the group membership of a white-collar employee supervisory board member changes to the white-collar employees defined in Art. 3, Section 3, No. 1 or the managerial white-collar employees.

Third Division
Internal Order, Rights and Duties of the Supervisory Board

Article 25
Basic Principle

(1) The internal order, decision-making process and the rights and duties of the supervisory board are determined ac-

cording to Articles 27 to 29, Articles 31 and 32 and, insofar as these provisions do not preclude their application

1. for joint stock companies and partnerships based on shares, according to the Joint Stock Company Act,
2. for limited-liability companies ["Gesellschaften mit beschränkter Haftung"] and companies in the form of a "Gewerkschaft" under mining statutes, according to Art. 90, Sections 3, 4 and 5, Sentences 1 and 2; Articles 107 to 116, 118, Section 2; Art. 125, Section 3; and Articles 171 and 268, Section 2, of the Joint Stock Company Act,
3. for profit-oriented economic cooperatives,according to the Act on Profit-oriented Economic Cooperatives.

Art. 4, Section 2 of the Act on Transferring Shareowner Rights in "Volkswagenwerk Gesellschaft mit beschränkter Haftung" into Private Possession of July 21, 1960 (Federal Law Gazette I p. 585), last amended by the Second Amendment Act to the Act on Transferring Shareowner Rights in "Volkswagenwerk Gesellschaft mit beschränkter Haftung" into Private Possession of July 31, 1970 (Federal Law Gazette I p. 1149), remains unaffected.

(2) Other legal directives and determinations of the bylaws (of the articles of partnership, of the statute) or the standing orders ["Geschäftsordnung"] of the supervisory board on the internal order, decision-making process and rights and duties of the supervisory board remain unaffected, insofar as this does not conflict with Section 1.

Article 26
Protection of Supervisory-Board Members Against Disadvantage

Jobholder supervisory-board members may not be disturbed or hindered in carrying out their activities. They may not be disadvantaged because of their activities in the supervisory board of the enterprise whose jobholders they are or, according to Art. 4 or Art. 5, are deemed to be. This applies also to their professional development.

Article 27
Chairmanship in the Supervisory Board

(1) The supervisory board elects from its midst, with a majority of two-thirds of the total number of members of which it must consist, one supervisory board chairman and one deputy.

(2) If the necessary majority according to Section 1 is not achieved in the election of the supervisory-board chairman or his deputy, a second ballot takes place to elect the supervisory-board chairman and his deputy. In this ballot, the shareholder supervisory-board members elect the supervisory-board chairman and the jobholder supervisory-board members elect the deputy, in each case with the majority of the votes cast.

(3) Immediately after the election of the supervisory-board chairman and his deputy, the supervisory board forms a committee to attend to the task defined in Art. 31, Section 3, Sentence 1; those belonging to the committee being the supervisory-board chairman, his deputy and, elected by the majority of the votes cast, one each of the jobholder supervisory-board members and the shareholder supervisory-board members.

Article 28
Quorum

The supervisory board is capable of making decisions only if at least half of the total number of members of which it must consist take part in the decision. Art. 108, Section 2, Sentence 4 of the Joint Stock Company Act applies.

Article 29
Voting

(1) Supervisory-board decisions require the majority of the votes cast, insofar as something different is not specified in Section 2, and in Articles 27, 31 and 32.

(2) If a supervisory-board ballot results in a tie, the supervisory-board chairman has two votes in a renewed ballot on the same issue if it also results in a tie. Art. 108, Section 3, of

the Joint Stock Company Act also applies to the casting of the second vote. The deputy is not entitled to the second vote.

Part Three
Organ Legally Representing the Enterprise

Article 30
Basic Principle

The composition, the rights and duties of the organ that is the legal representative of the enterprise and the appointment of its members are determined according to the provisions bearing on the legal form of the enterprise, insofar as Articles 31 to 33 specify nothing different.

Article 31
Appointment and Revocation

(1) The appointment of the members of the organ that is the legal representative of the enterprise and the revocation of the appointment are determined according to Articles 84 and 85 of the Joint Stock Company Act, insofar as they do not conflict with Sections 2 to 5. This does not apply for partnerships based on shares.

(2) The supervisory board appoints the members of the organ that is the legal representative of the enterprise with a majority that includes at least two-thirds of the votes of its members.

(3) If no appointment can be made according to Section 2, the supervisory-board committee designated in Art. 27, Section 3, must make an appointment proposal to the supervisory board within one month after the ballot in which the majority prescribed in Section 2 was not achieved; this proposal does not exclude other proposals. The supervisory board appoints the members of the organ that is the legal representative of the enterprise with the majority of the votes of its members.

(4) If no appointment can be made according to Section 3, the supervisory-board chairman has two votes in a renewed

ballot; Section 3, Sentence 2, applies. Art. 108, Section 3, of the Joint Stock Company Act applies to the casting of the second vote. The deputy is not entitled to the second vote.

(5) Sections 2 to 4 apply accordingly to the revocation of the appointment of a member of the organ that is the legal representative of the enterprise.

Article 32
Exercise of Participation Rights

(1) The organ that is the legal representative of an enterprise in which the jobholders have co-determination rights according to this law can exercise the following rights having their source in share ownership in another enterprise, whose jobholders have co-determination rights according to this law, only on the basis of prior decisions of the supervisory board: pertaining to the appointment, the revocation of the appointment or approval of the conduct of business of members of statutory organs of the enterprise as well as to decisions on liquidating, merging or changing organization form of the other enterprise; to the conclusion of intercompany contracts (Articles 291, 292 of the Joint Stock Company Act) with the other enterprise; to its continuation after liquidation or to transferring its assets. These decisions require only the majority of the votes of the shareholder supervisory-board members; they are binding on the organ that is the legal representative of the enterprise.

(2) Section 1 does not apply if the participation of the enterprise in the other enterprise amounts to less than one quarter.

Article 33
Labor Director ["Arbeitsdirektor"]

(1) A labor director shall be appointed as an equally entitled member of the organ that is the legal representative of the enterprise. This does not apply to partnerships based on shares.

(2) Like the other members of the organ that is the legal representative of the enterprise, the labor director must carry

out his tasks in the closest accord with the organ as a whole. Particulars are determined by the standing orders.

(3) In the case of profit-oriented trading cooperatives, Art. 9, Section 2 of the Act on Profit-Oriented Economic Cooperatives does not apply to the labor director.

Part Four
Merchant Shipping

Article 34

(1) All the ships of an enterprise are regarded as one facility in applying this act.

(2) Ships within the meaning of the act are merchant vessels sailing under the federal flag according to the Flag Act. Ships which, as a rule, return to the site of an on-land facility within 48 hours of putting to sea, are considered a part of this on-land facility.

(3) In a facility designated in Section 1, only the masters of the ships are managerial white-collar employees within the meaning of Art. 3, Section 3, No. 2 of this act.

(4) Jobholders of a facility designated in Section 1 do not take part in a vote according to Art. 9 and do not come into consideration in computing the number of jobholders required to submit applications and make decisions.

(5) If the jobholder supervisory-board members are elected by electors, then, deviating from Art. 10, no electors are elected in a facility designated in Section 1. Deviating from Art. 15, Section 1, the jobholders of this facility participate directly in the election of the jobholder supervisory-board members, with the proviso

1. that the vote of one of these jobholders should be counted as one-sixtieth of an elector's vote; Art. 11, Section 1, Sentence 3 applies accordingly;
2. that these jobholders do not take part in voting on the joint election by the electors of the jobholder supervisory board members and do not come into consideration in computing the numbers of blue-collar worker electors and white-collar

employee electors required to submit applications and make decisions.

(6) If the jobholder supervisory-board members are elected in direct elections, and if no more than one-tenth of the jobholders of the enterprise belong to a facility designated in Sentence 1, these jobholders do not take part in a vote on the joint election of the jobholder supervisory-board members and do not come into consideration in computing the number of blue-collar workers and white-collar employees required to submit applications and make decisions.

Part Five
Transitional and Final Provisions

Article 35
Amendments and Repeal of Acts

[This article, consisting of instructions for altering other laws to make them conform with the new law, is meaningless when read by itself. For this reason, it has been omitted from this translation.]

Article 36
References

(1) Insofar as references are made in other provisions to the provisions of the Works Constitution Act of 1952 concerning the representation of jobholders in the supervisory boards of enterprises, these references are considered as references to this act with respect to companies designated in Art. 1, Section 1, of this act.

(2) Insofar as in other provisions the designation "Co-determination Act" is used for the Act on Co-determination by Jobholders in the Supervisory and Management Boards of Mining, Iron and Steel Industry Enterprises of May 21, 1951 (Federal Law Gazette I p. 347), last amended by the Introductory Act to the Joint Stock Company Act of September 6, 1965 (Federal

Law Gazette I p. 1185), it is replaced by the designation "Mining, Iron and Steel Industry Co-determination Act."

Article 37
First Application of the Act to an Enterprise

(1) Stipulations that are not compatible with the provisions of this act in the bylaws (in the articles of association, in the statute), other than those designated in Art. 97, Section 2, Sentence 2, of the Joint Stock Company Act, go out of force at the point in time designated in Art. 97, Section 2, Sentence 2, or, in the case of a court decision, at the point in time designated in Art. 98, Section 4, Sentence 2 of the Joint Stock Company Act. A shareholders' meeting (meeting of partners, meeting of shareholders of a "Gewerkschaft" under mining statutes, a general shareholders' meeting) which takes place up to this point in time, can decide with a simple majority on new bylaw stipulations to replace those going out of force.

(2) Articles 25 to 29, 31 to 33 are to be used for the first time when the supervisory board is composed according to the provisions of this law.

(3) Where a member has been appointed before the effective date of this act to serve on the organ authorized for legal representation of an enterprise immediately subject to this act when it comes into force, his appointment can—insofar as the term of office of this member does not end sooner for other reasons—be revoked by the supervisory board formed under this act, at any time after five years have elapsed since this act came into force. The revocation requires the majority of the votes cast by the supervisory-board members, all the votes of the shareholder supervisory-board members or all the votes of the jobholder supervisory-board members. General provisions apply for claims arising from the employment contract. Up to revocation, bylaw specifications concerning the term of office remain in force for these members, deviating from Section 1, Sentence 1. These provisions shall apply accordingly if the first time this act is applied to an enterprise occurs only after it has taken effect.

(4) Section 3 does not apply to personally liable partners of a partnership based on shares.

Article 38
Transitional Provision

(1) In the first two years after this act takes effect, the point in time stipulated in Art. 97, Section 2, Sentence 2, of the Joint Stock Company Act for its first application to an enterprise is replaced by the end of the second shareholders' meeting (meeting of partners, meeting of shareholders of a "Gewerkschaft" under mining statutes, general shareholders' meeting) to be called after the act takes effect, though this may not be later than the day on which two years have elapsed since the act took effect. Sentence 1 shall not apply if the point in time specified in Art. 97, Section 2, Sentence 2, of the Joint Stock Company Act is later than the point in time specified in Sentence 1. Deviating from Sentence 1, the first shareholders' meeting (meeting of partners, meeting of shareholders in a "Gewerkschaft" under mining statutes, general shareholders' meeting) to be called after this act takes effect may specify an earlier point in time.

(2) If, in the first two years after this act comes into force, a court decision under Art. 98 of the Joint Stock Company Act rules that the supervisory board is to be composed according to the provisions of this act, then the point in time specified in Art. 98, Section 4, Sentence 2, Art. 97, Section 2, Sentence 2, of the Joint Stock Company Act is replaced by the end of the next shareholders' meeting (meeting of partners, meeting of shareholders of a "Gewerkschaft" under mining statutes, general shareholders' meeting) to be called after the effective date of the court decision, so long as at least six months elapse between the effective date and the calling of the meeting; if this period is less than six months, then the point in time specified in Art. 98, Section 4, Sentence 2, Art. 97, Section 2, Sentence 2, of the Joint Stock Company Act is replaced by the end of the second shareholders' meeting (meeting of partners, meeting of shareholders of a "Gewerkschaft" under mining statutes, general shareholders' meeting) to be called after the effective date of the court decision, but no later than the day on which one year has elapsed since the court decision took effect.

(3) If, in the first two years after this act takes effect, court proceedings are initiated under Art. 97 or Art. 98 of the Joint Stock Company Act with the aim of having the supervisory

board composed according to the provisions of this act, then the term of office of jobholder supervisory board members elected under Art. 76 of the Works Constitution Act of 1952 is extended until the start of the term of office of the jobholder supervisory-board members who are to be elected once the court proceedings have ended; however, this extension may not go beyond the point in time stipulated in Section 1, in the case of Art. 97 of the Joint Stock Company Act, and Section 2, in the case of Art. 98 of the Joint Stock Company Act. Should the court rule that the supervisory board is not to be composed according to the provisions of this act, then the term of office expires no later than the point in time stipulated in Art. 98, Section 4, Sentence 2, of the Joint Stock Company Act.

Article 39
Authorization to Issue Regulations

The Federal Government is authorized to issue regulations concerning the process for electing and dismissing supervisory-board members, in particular concerning

1. the preparation of the election or vote, the appointment of election committees as well as the drawing up of voter lists,
2. votes on whether supervisory board members shall be elected directly or through electors, and on whether joint elections shall take place,
3. the time limit for the examination of voter lists and the raising of objections,
4. the computation of the number of jobholder supervisory-board members as well as their apportionment among the blue-collar workers, the white-collar employees defined in Art. 3, Section 3, No. 1, the managerial white-collar employees, and the union representatives.
5. the computation of the number of electors as well as their apportionment among the blue-collar workers, the white-collar employees defined in Art. 3, Section 3, No. 1 and the managerial white-collar employees,
6. the election candidate lists and the deadline for their submission,

7. the calling of the election or the vote and the time limit for making the calling of the election publicly known,
8. the participation in elections and votes of jobholders of a facility designated in Art. 34, Section 1,
9. the casting of votes,
10. the determination of the result of the election or vote and the time limits for its publication,
11. the safeguarding of election documents and voting documents.

Article 40
Berlin Clause

This act applies also in the State of Berlin pursuant to Art. 13, Section 1, of the Third Transitional Act of Jan. 4, 1952 (Federal Law Gazette I p. 1). Regulations based on this Act apply in the State of Berlin according to Art. 14 of the Third Transitional Act.

Article 41
Effective Date

This Act comes into force on July 1, 1976.

[End of Act]

—Translation by Roon Lewald and James Furlong—

Footnotes to Chapter 1

1. *Handelsblatt,* news item dated April 10-11, 1976.
2. *Die Mitbestimmung der Arbeitnehmer,* Bonn, German Federal Ministry of Labor, 1974, p. 20.
3. Karl Fitting, Otfried Wlotzke, Hellmut Wissmann; *Mitbestimmungsgesetz, Kommentar,* Munich, Verlag Franz Vahlen, 1976, p. 28. This book, written by three Labor Ministry officials, is a definitive explanation of the new law.
4. Robert Ball, "The Hard Hats in Europe's Boardrooms," *Fortune,* June 1976.
5. Werner Hansen, *Mitbestimmung der Arbeitnehmer, ein Leitfaden,* Düsseldorf, DGB Vorstand, 1968, p. 10.
6. Erich Potthoff, "Zur Geschichte der Mitbestimmung," from *Zwischenbilanz der Mitbestimmung,* by Potthoff, Otto Blume and Otto Duvernall, Tübingen, Hans-Bockler-Gesellschaft, 1962.
7. Hansen, op. cit., p. 12.
8. Press release, "Chemie zur Mitbestimmung Nr. 4," Frankfurt, Verband der Chemischen Industrie e.V. and Arbeitsring der Arbeitgeberverbände der Deutschen Chemischen Industrie e.V., 1970.
9. Helmut Schmidt, "Die Mitbestimmung der Arbeitnehmer—von Adenauer als eine der grossen Aufgaben unserer Zeit verstanden," reprint from *Konrad Adenauer und Seine Zeit,* 1976, Deutsche Verlags-Anstalt GmbH.
10. Ibid.
11. Ibid.
12. *Das Mitbestimmungsgespräch,* No. 2, 1975.
13. News release by the German Federal Press Office, Feb. 20, 1974.
14. Martin Peltzer, *Co-Determination Bill, 1974,* Cologne, Verlag Dr. Otto Schmidt, p. 21.
15. AP-Dow Jones News Service Oct. 15, 1974.
16. Matthöfer remarks to Bonn American Businessmen's Club, Jan. 8, 1976.
17. *Frankfurter Allgemeine Zeitung* March 27, 1976.
18. Press conference of American Chamber of Commerce in Germany, Frankfurt, March 26, 1976.
19. German service of the Associated Press March 29, 1976.
20. Helmut Schmidt, *Bundestags Reden und Zeitdokumente,* Bonn, Verlag az studio bonn, 1975, p. 85.
21. *Das Mitbestimmungsgespräch,* No. 9-10, 1975.
22. Hansen, op. cit., pp. 8-9.
23. Stenographic record Oct. 16, 1974, hearings of Bundestag Labor and Social Committee, Drucksache 7/2172, p.16.
24. *Das Mitbestimmungsgespräch* No. 9-10, 1975.
25. Ibid.

General Note: Messrs. Grünewald, Fitting, Walther, Baker, Pfromm, Frerk and Siemon were interviewed.

Footnotes to Chapter 2

1. *Bild,* 17 May 1976.
2. Stenographic record Oct. 16, 1974, hearings of Bundestag Labor and Social Committee, Drucksache 7/2172, p. 51.
3. Friedrich Kübel, *Das Mitbestimmungsgespräch,* No. 5-7, 1976.
4. Stenographic record, op. cit., p.23.
5. Ibid., p. 26.
6. Kurt H. Biedenkopf et al., *Mitbestimmung in Unternehmen,* Parliamentary Report, Drucksache VI/334, 1970, p. 92.
7. Stenographic record, op. cit., p. 50.
8. Heiner Radzio (ed.), *Warum Mitbestimmung und wie?* Düsseldorf: Econ Verlag, 1970, p. 44.
9. Ibid., p.41.
10. Biedenkopf Report, op. cit., pp 14-15.
11. Ibid., p. 47.
12. Stenographic record, op. cit., pp. 23, 54-55.
13. Helmut Kater, *Das Mitbestimmungsgespräch,* op. cit.
14. Stenographic record, op. cit., p. 16.
15. Ibid., p. 58.
16. Gerhard Leminsky, *Das Mitbestimmungsgespräch,* op. cit.
17. Ernst Viebahn, *Das Mitbestimmungsgespräch,* op. cit.
18. Stenographic record Nov. 4, 1974, hearings of Bundestag Labor and Social Committee, Parliamentary Report, Drucksache 7/2172, p.44.
19. Ibid., p. 48.
20. Alfred L. Thimm, *Decision-Making at Volkswagen 1972-1975,* revised edition, Schenectady, Union College and University, Institute of Administration and Management, February 1976, pp. 28-29.
21. Paul Kemezis, "Keeping Labor Peace in Germany," *New York Times,* April 11, 1976.
22. *Handelsblatt,* "Schmückers Weichen: Vom Aufsichtsrat gestellt," article dated April 26, 1976.

Footnotes to Chapter 3

1. Figures supplied by the German Labor Union Federation.
2. Remarks at Bonn American Businessman's Club, April 13, 1976.
3. *Bericht des Ausschusses für Arbeit und Sozialordnung,* Drucksache 7/4845, Bonn, Bonner Universitäts-Buchdruckerei, 1976, p. 5.
4. Hans-Christoph Leo, "Epochale Bedeutung," (Part 2), *Manager Magazin,* July 1976.
5. *Handelsblatt,* April 13, 1976.
6. Press release "Mischnick: Die Neue Unternehmungsverfassung—Kooperation Statt Konfrontation," press service of the Free Democratic Party's Bundestag members, Jan. 7, 1976.

7. Hans-Christoph Leo, "Epochale Bedeutung" (Part I), *Manager Magazin,* June 1976.
8. *Stellungnahme des Arbeitskreises Mitbestimmung zum Mitbestimmungs-Gesetz* Cologne, Bundesvereinigung der Deutschen Arbeitgeberverbände, 1976, p. 8.
9. *Bericht des Auschusses,* op. cit., pp. 8-9.
10. Press release "Interview mit Graf Lambsdorff zum Neuen Mitbestimmungsgesetz," FDP press service, June 30, 1976.
11. *Stellungnahme des Arbeitskreises Mitbestimmung,* op. cit., p. 18.
12. *Handelsblatt,* Article dated July 16-17, 1976.
13. Hans-Jochen Vogel, "Macht über Menschen bedarf der Legitimation," *Manager Magazin,* July 1976, p. 18.
14. *Mitbestimmung, Sozialdemokratische Fachkonferenz,* Bonn, Vorstand der SPD, Göttinger Druckerei und Verlagsgesellschaft mbh, 1976, pp. 16-17.
15. Stenographic Record Oct. 16, 1974 hearings of Bundestag Labor and Social Committee, Drucksache 7/2172, p.15.

Footnotes to Chapter 4

1. P. L. Davies, "European Experience with Worker Representation on the Board," from *Industrial Democracy, European Experience,* London, Her Majesty's Stationery Office, 1976.
2. *Employee Participation and Company Structure, Bulletin of the European Communities, Supplement 8/75,* Brussels, European Communities Commission, 1975.
3. *Act on Co-Determination at Work,* SAF translation, Doc No. 1532, Stockholm, 1976.
4. *Constitution of the Swedish Employers' Confederation with Amendments Passed by the General Assembly Prior to and at Its Session of June 25, 1964.* Stockholm 1972.
5. Lennart Grafström, "Board Representation for Employees in Sweden," Stockholm, SAF, May 25, 1976.
6. "Wage Earner Funds," SAF Doc No 1446 (I), Stockholm 1976.
7. "Supplementary Note of Evidence by the TUC General Council in Elucidation of the TUC Statement *Industrial Democracy* and Related Questions Being Considered by the Bullock Committee," London, TUC, 1976.
8. Press release, "Mr. Peter Shore Announces Membership of Committee of Inquiry on Industrial Democracy," Department of Trade, London, Dec. 3, 1975.
9. Supplementary Note, op. cit.
10. "The Full Text of CBI's Evidence to the Bullock Committee of Enquiry Into Industrial Democracy March 1976," London, Confederation of British Industry, 1976.
11. *The Reform of the Enterprise in France (English Translation of the "Sudreau Report"),* Philadelphia, The Wharton School Industrial Research Unit, 1975.

12. Ibid., p. 99.
13. Ibid., p. 81.
14. Hanns Neuerbourg, "Co-Determination," Associated Press news dispatch, 16 March 1976.

General note: Mrs. Isaksson and Messrs. Lidbom, Bergqvist, Grafström, Robertson, Lea, Hawksworth and Condon were interviewed.

Footnotes to Chapter 5

1. Article by Neil McInnes carried by AP-Dow Jones News Service, July 10, 1976.
2. Robert Ball, "The Hard Hats in Europe's Boardrooms," *Fortune,* June 1976.
3. Quoted by AP-Dow Jones News Service, July 27, 1976.
4. William Matthewson, "The French Penchant for Hiring M.B.A.s From American Schools Seems to Fade," *The Wall Street Journal,* Aug 24, 1976.

General Note: Messrs. Brown, Dale and Rebhan were interviewed by telephone.

Index